Planet of
the Apes™
Collectibles

Unauthorized Guide with Trivia & Values

Christopher R. Sausville

4880 Lower Valley Road, Atglen, PA 19310 USA

Dedication

This book is dedicated to my wife, Frances, whose perseverance, support, and love made this book possible. I thank her for all the countless hours she has spent with me watching the films, reading my draft copies, traveling to toy shows, and taking telephone calls at all hours of the night from ape collectors throughout the country. She has always supported my determination to produce this book and the enjoyment I receive from collecting *Planet of the Apes* memorabilia. She inspired me to follow my dream to produce this book and I am forever grateful.

I would also like to make a special dedication to the memory of my parents, Ralph and Barbara Sausville. They always supported my endeavors and taught me the importance of working hard to achieve my goals. I wish they could have been here to share this special moment with me.

Published by Schiffer Publishing Ltd.
4880 Lower Valley Road
Atglen, PA 19310
Phone: (610) 593-1777; Fax: (610) 593-2002
E-mail: schifferbk@aol.com
Please write for a free catalog.
This book may be purchased from the publisher.
Please include $3.95 for shipping.
Try your bookstore first.

We are interested in hearing from authors
with book ideas on related subjects.

Notice of Copyright Ownership

Planet of the Apes; Twentieth Century-Fox Film Corporation
Planet of the Apes; APJAC Productions, Ltd.

Disclaimer: This *Planet of the Apes Trivia Book and Collectibles Guide* is an unauthorized, independent study by the author, Christopher R. Sausville. The research of this book was not sponsored in any way by the manufacturer of the items featured in this book. The photographs utilized in the trivia section are copyright of Twentieth Century-Fox Film Corporation. The prices listed are intended as value guides rather than set prices. The values quoted are as accurate as possible, but in the case of errors, neither the author nor the publisher assumes liability for any loss incurred by the use of this book.

Contents

Acknowledgments

There are several people who have been a great help in preparing this book. I am grateful to my fellow ape collectors: Matthew Sotis, Joe Farr, and Anthony George. They have all shared the same passion for *Planet of the Apes* that drives me and have been instrumental in helping me gather information on *Planet of the Apes* memorabilia. They have also contributed to the growth of my collection. I have learned a great deal from them about ape collectibles and I always enjoy chatting with them about *Planet of the Apes*. I especially want to thank Matthew Sotis for the use of his custom figure and mask photos.

I'm also grateful to my brother, Mark Sausville, who introduced me to *Planet of the Apes* when I was young and shares a common fondness for the subject. He has been my collecting companion since I started over four years ago. There were two instances involving my brother that started the collecting frenzy for me. First, a trip he took to Texas where he saw the television commercial in which he noticed the ape model kits. Second, his discovery of Joey Ferro's science-fiction store in Schenectady, New York, where I was able to obtain several pieces for my collection. It was after my initial visit to Ferro's store, and the discovery of *Toy Shop Magazine,* that I began my all out quest to collect *Planet of the Apes* memorabilia.

I want to thank the late Arthur P. Jacobs. If it wasn't for his drive and determination to get the *Planet of the Apes* movie made, there wouldn't be any memorabilia to collect. I am grateful to my longtime friend Phil Cortese for the use of his camera, as well as his assistance and patience in taking pictures of all of my collectibles for this book. Lastly, I want to thank Schiffer Publishing for having faith in my idea and Jeff Snyder for all his help in organizing the book. Without all their contributions, this book would not be as thorough or complete and I would not have been able to realize my dream of having it published.

```
                    "PLANET OF THE APES"

        FADE IN

   1    EXT. CONSTELLATION OF ORION - NIGHT

        Stars glitter like diamonds on the black velvet backdrop
        of space.  The Belt of Orion is center screen, but much
        nearer and larger than ever seen by an Earth-bound
        astronomer.

        A speck of light appears in the lower left corner of the
        screen.  No spaceship can be seen, but only a glowworm,
        a solitary spermatosoan gliding through the womb of the
        universe.  Over this we HEAR the voice of an astronaut.
        He is concluding a report.

                        ASTRONAUT'S VOICE
                            (o.s.)
                So ends my last signal until we reach
                our destination.  We are now on
                automatic, a mere hundred and five
                light years from our base...and at the
                mercy of computers.  I've tucked in my
                crew for the long sleep.  I'll join
                them presently.

   2    INT. CABIN OF SPACESHIP - ESTABLISHING SHOT - NIGHT

        The cabin is neither cramped nor spacious, but about the
        size of the President's cabin in Air Force One.  In the
        immediate f.g. is a console of dials and switches
        flanked by four chairs.  Only one of the chairs is
        occupied.  The astronaut's back is to CAMERA.  There is
        a ladder amidships which leads to an escape hatch.  The
        after part of the cabin is obscured in darkness.  We
        hear the MUSIC of a Mozart sonata emanating from a
        phonograph of stereotape.  The astronaut is speaking into
        a microphone.

                        ASTRONAUT
                Within the hour we shall complete
                the sixth month of our flight from
                Cape Kennedy.  By our time, that is...

        He pauses, looking up at:

   3    TWO LARGE CLOCKS - ON CABIN WALL

        One clock is marked SELF TIME, but instead of twelve
        numerals it has twenty-four.  One of the needles is
        moving very slowly.

                                                Cont.

        NOTE:  THIS IS THE FIRST PAGE OF THE MAY 5, 1967 SHOOTING SCRIPT.
```

Introduction

"Hurtled some 2,000 years through time and space, four American astronauts, sleeping in a state of suspended animation, crash-land in the wilderness of an unidentified planet when their spacecraft suffers a navigational malfunction." This is how James Denton, Director of Publicity for *Planet of the Apes*, describes the beginning for one of the greatest science-fiction films of all time, *Planet of the Apes*.

He further noted in the *Final Production Information Guide on Planet of the Apes* that the film catapults the viewer into a strange simian civilization where man is regarded as a brute to be controlled and contained unless he grow in numbers and strength and ultimately destroy the ape culture and society. It is unlikely that anyone who has seen *Planet of the Apes* will ever forget the experience.[1]

A fascinating commentary on man's entrance into the space age can be found in *Planet of the Apes*. Pierre Boulle uses man's newfound ability to leave Earth as a spring board for his story and probes into the mysteries of what man may eventually find in outer space and on other worlds. While the film can be categorized as science-fiction, it also provides a stimulus for many provocative thoughts on man's past, present, and future.[2] To this day it remains one of the greatest films ever made and it is considered a classic in the science-fiction genre. With its fantastic makeup effects, bone chilling musical score, and shocking climax, *Planet of the Apes* drops the viewer onto a strange world and then takes him on a fantastic expedition into the future.

As this science-fiction classic approaches its thirtieth anniversary, and with rumors of the possible release of a new apes film, I felt the time was right to take you on a journey into the Forbidden Zone and beyond. With the increased popularity in the science-fiction genre, as well as the great demand for collectible toys and memorabilia from science-fiction films, it will be an opportune time to rekindle some childhood memories for many people. There is also no time like the present to introduce a whole new generation of people to what many consider the greatest film ever made. I have seen other collectible books which mention *Planet of the Apes*, but none have been as comprehensive, detailed, and up-to-date as this one.

My intention was not only to produce a book on collectibles, but also to incorporate a concept that would be both challenging and fun. Therefore, I included a section on trivia and facts from the original *Planet of the Apes* film. After approximately 30 minutes of wondering what the astronauts will find on this desolate planet, you finally realize they have landed on a planet ruled by talking, intelligent apes. From the moment the camera swung from a tight shot of Taylor ducking into the cornfield, to the classic, close-up shot of the soldier ape on horseback during the hunt scene, I was hooked on *Planet of the Apes*. Over the past four years, I have become an avid *Planet of the Apes* collector and thought people would be interested in testing their knowledge on trivia and facts from the first film in addition to being provided insight into the world of ape collectibles.

Before we get started with the trivia questions on the original *Planet of the Apes* film, let's take a journey into Ape City for a synopsis of the ape movies, television series, and the animated cartoon. The first film, *Planet of the Apes*, premiered on February 8, 1968, and was welcomed by the public with open arms. The concept of a planet run by talking, intelligent apes, where humans are considered the lowest primate on the evolutionary chain, intrigued audiences throughout the world. The film received great reviews and broke box-office records wherever it was shown. Besides being such a huge hit, it also created a new film genre, the space opera, which grew to tremendous proportions with the release of such films as *Close Encounters of the Third Kind* and *Star Wars*. To prevent giving away any of the answers to the trivia questions, we will not go into detail about the first film. Following the great success of *Planet of the Apes*, it was decided that a sequel was required. Although Arthur Jacobs was apprehensive about making a sequel, Richard Zanuck at 20th Century-Fox convinced him to film one. *Beneath the Planet of the Apes* (originally titled *Planet of the Apes Revisited*) was released in 1970 and it was immediately embraced by the movie audience, providing another hit film for the producers.

The astronauts prepare for their mission in *Planet of the Apes*.

When originally approached to reprise his role as Taylor, Charlton Heston was not overly enthusiastic about the idea, but felt he owed Arthur Jacobs and Richard Zanuck a favor. He wanted to be killed off in the opening scene, but it was eventually decided that he would disappear into the Forbidden Zone at the beginning of the film and be killed in the end. He accepted this idea, but did not accept a fee for his role. Instead, he had his salary donated to his son's school. This film picks up where *Planet* left off as Taylor and Nova (Linda Harrison) travel into the Forbidden Zone. Once in the Forbidden Zone, unusual events (mirages of fire, lightning, and an earthquake) occur and Taylor disappears into thin air. James Franciscus stars as Astronaut Brent, who is sent from present day Earth to find Taylor. After crashing on the planet, Brent eventually meets up with Nova, who takes him to Ape City to meet Cornelius and Zira. They arrive while General Ursus (James Gregory) is addressing the Ape Council about taking a journey into the Forbidden Zone. The film builds up with anticipation and concludes with a climactic battle between the apes, led by Dr. Zaius (Maurice Evans) & General Ursus, and the mutant humans, who dwell under the ruins of New York City and worship a nuclear bomb as their God. The stunning ending, with its Doomsday Bomb detonation, left no room for another movie; yet, the creative mind of Paul Dehn came up with a concept for a third film.

General Ursus and Dr. Zaius lead the gorilla soldiers into the Forbidden Zone and a confrontation with the mutant humans in *Beneath the Planet of the Apes*.

The third installment in the apes saga was *Escape from the Planet of the Apes* (1971) (originally titled *Secret of the Planet of the Apes*), where Doctors Cornelius, Zira, and Milo travel back in time to Earth 1974 in Taylor's salvaged spacecraft. The spacecraft crashes into the sea and the apes are greeted to Earth by a society of talking humans. Initially, the humans treat the talking apes like celebrities, as they are wined, dined, and living a life of luxury in the most expensive hotel. This lavish lifestyle does not last long as a plot to kill the talking apes is devised when it is learned that Zira is pregnant. The threat of a baby ape who could speak sends the world into a frenzy. The movie skillfully mixes humor, social commentary, and suspense. *Escape* sets the stage for the remaining films with the birth of baby Milo to Cornelius and Zira. Before they are eventually killed, Cornelius and Zira smuggle the baby chimpanzee into a traveling circus run by Armando (Ricardo Montalban), a kind circus owner who loves all animals.

Drs. Cornelius, Zira, and Milo are greeted to planet Earth circa 1975 in *Escape from the Planet of the Apes*.

The fourth film, *Conquest of the Planet of the Apes* (1972), takes place on North America in 1991 after Milo (with his name changed to Caesar) has grown up. After spending his whole life secluded in the traveling circus, he is introduced to society by Armando. At this time, a plague from space brought back by astronauts has wiped out all the cats and dogs in the world. The apes have, at first, taken their place as household pets. With their advanced intelligence, however, the apes are soon elevated to the position of servants by the humans. The humans continually mistreat the apes until Caesar leads the apes' revolt against their human masters. Caesar escapes electrocution with the help of MacDonald (Hari Rhodes), a human who sympathizes with the ape's plea. Caesar is ordered to be executed by Governor Breck (Don Murray), but MacDonald intervenes by turning off the power to the electrical system prior to the electrocution. The film contains a thrilling ending in which the apes take over the city and Caesar makes his climactic speech claiming the world is now going to be run by a planet of apes.

The final film in the apes saga was *Battle for the Planet of the Apes* (1973). This film (originally titled *Epic of the Planet of the Apes*) was set in 2670 AD, following the destruction of society by the dropping of the bomb. It was a narrative story introduced by the Lawgiver (John Huston). It focuses on Caesar's leadership over a peaceful village where apes and humans live and work together. The film stars Claude Akins as General Aldo, the head of the gorillas, who leads a rebellion against Caesar (Roddy McDowall), because he refuses to live peacefully with the humans. The story also involves the discovery of an underground society of mutant humans, who plan to wage war against the ape village. The film includes a great battle scene, and con-

Caesar leads the ape's revolt in *Conquest of the Planet of the Apes.*

cludes with the apes driving the remaining mutant humans back to their underground habitat. The film also includes Caesar's revenge for the death of his son, Cornelius, during a confrontation with General Aldo, who was responsible for young Cornelius' demise. After the smoke clears, there is a new beginning of hope for the apes and humans as they begin to rebuild their village.

General Aldo is confronted by Caesar in *Battle for the Planet of the Apes.*

The next stop for the apes was on television. A weekly hour-long television series, devised by Anthony Wilson and produced by Herbert Hirschman and Stan Hough, appeared Friday evenings on CBS. The show premiered on September 13, 1974, and followed the journeys of Astronauts Peter Burke (James Naughton) and Alan Virdon (Ron Harper) after they crash-land on Earth in the year 3085 AD. They struggle to stay one step ahead of General Urko (Mark Lenard), the leader of the gorillas, and Dr. Zaius (Booth Coleman), the Chief Minister of Science. The humans are befriended by a sympathetic chimpanzee named Galen (Roddy McDowall), who aids them in their search for a way off the planet. The fourteen episode series tracks the astronauts adventures on the simian ruled planet as they travel to different ape villages and encounter new situations each week. A listing of each episode can be found in the collectibles section of the book. Also, you can find a listing of the five, two-hour made for television movies for the *Planet of the Apes*. These movies were, in fact, the one-hour television series spliced together into two-hour television movies and sold to different stations for syndication.

Galen, Burke, and Virdon in a scene from the *Planet of the Apes* television series.

Following the cancellation of the television series, an animated cartoon was released on September 6, 1975, entitled *Return to the Planet of the Apes*. The premise of the cartoon, which was produced by Dave DePatie and Friz Freleng, involved three American astronauts (Bill Hudson, Jeff Allen, and Judy Franklin) who travel from Earth time 1975 to Earth time 3979 AD. Upon landing on the planet, they discover a world ruled by intelligent apes, where humans are treated as the lesser species (pets, servants, and sport for hunters). The stranded astronauts seek refuge in a colony of mute humans called New City. Following a raid of the colony by the apes, Bill is captured and taken to Cornelius and Zira for experiments. It is then that Bill speaks, shocking the apes. The thirteen episodes follow the astronauts' adventures on the *Planet of the Apes* as they try to stay alive and find a way back to the Earth of their time. Unlike the films and television series, the cartoon displays an advanced, technology driven ape society, where they live in large cities and drive automobiles. This was the premise introduced in the original novel, but from which the films deviated. A listing of each *Return to the Planet of the Apes* episode can be found in the collectibles section of this book.

It has been over twenty years since a new ape product has been released. This may all change with the rumor that a new feature film is in the making. The advanced word on the film, which Oliver Stone is alleged to be producing, is that it will not be a remake of the original film, but will present a entirely new concept. The plot will apparently involve some kind of manipulation of genetic codes by intelligent apes at the dawn of mankind, which will result in dire consequences for present day civilization. The script, entitled *The Return of the Apes*, was written by Terry Hayes (*The Road Warrior*). A release date has not been set, but it is rumored that the film is in pre-production. We will have to wait and see what transpires.

The time has come to test your knowledge on one of the most successful and popular science-fiction movies in the history of film, the original *Planet of the Apes*. Take your time and read each question carefully, because if you get too many answers wrong, you will be summoned to the Forbidden Zone or caged like a human beast. The questions in this trivia book range in difficulty from easy questions for the novice to extremely difficult ones for the true apes fan. Begin your journey by watching the movie, paying close attention to detail, and *then* break out the book to test your knowledge on over 250 trivia questions from the film. Don't cheat and watch the movie *while* completing this quiz. Of course, there are a few questions concerning the other apes films, just to make things interesting.

Also, challenge your friends to see who the true apes fans are. Be warned that there are several questions whose answers do not appear in the film, so you will have to be familiar with behind the scenes action and facts as well. Good luck, human!

Bill, Nova, and Cornelius with a background of General Urko's head from *Return to the Planet of the Apes* animated cartoon.

Planet of the Apes Trivia

Background Trivia

1. Which apes film did Roddy McDowall *not* act in?
2. Who portrayed Roddy McDowall's character in the above film?
3. Natalie Trundy, who was married to Arthur Jacobs, appeared in all but one of the ape films. Do you know which film she did *not* appear in?
4. There were two people who appeared in all five of the ape films. Can you name them?
5. What is the title of the novel upon which *Planet of the Apes* is based?
6. Who is the author of this novel?
7. What other novel is this author famous for writing?
8. An honorary Academy Award was given to whom for his fantastic makeup design in *Planet of the Apes*?
9. The musical score for *Planet of the Apes*, which was nominated for an Academy Award, was composed by whom?
10. What two writers are credited with writing the screenplay for the film?
11. Before Charlton Heston obtained the starring role as Taylor, several other actors were considered for this role. Can you name the three primary actors considered?
12. Who was originally cast to play Dr. Zaius, but had to withdraw for health reasons?
13. Who ultimately played the role of Dr. Zaius?
14. Whose tireless effort was instrumental in the apes making it to the big screen?
15. How did the above person eventually convince the executives at 20th Century-Fox to fund the movie?
16. Do you know the name of the top executive at 20th Century-Fox who gave Arthur Jacobs the "green light" to make *Planet of the Apes*?
17. Four people appeared in the screen test for the film. Can you name them?
18. What characters were portrayed in the screen test?
19. Who directed *Planet of the Apes*?
20. Who produced *Planet of the Apes*?
21. What are the three different classifications of apes in *Planet of the Apes*?
22. What function do each of these apes play on the *Planet of the Apes*?
23. Who represents the lowest class of ape?
24. What other member of the ape family was included in one of the early drafts for the film, but was later removed?
25. At what level of the ape chain would these removed apes have ranked?
26. Taylor was not the original name selected for that character. What name originally appeared in the script and was also used for the screen test?
27. Do you know which chilling score was not included on the original soundtrack for *Planet of the Apes*, but was later added to the soundtrack when released by Intrada on compact disc?

28. In addition to the musical score, *Planet of the Apes* was also nominated for an Academy Award in another category. Who was nominated and what were they nominated for?
29. This *Planet of the Apes* actor's son starred on the television show *Wings*. Can you name the actor from *Wings*, as well his father and the role he played in *Planet of the Apes*? Think hard.
30. This one is for the die hard ape fan. Do you know the catch phrase used for *Planet of the Apes* in the trailer for the film?
31. What Academy Award winning cinematographer was the director of photography in *Planet of the Apes*?

Monkey Planet

As you know, or learned from a previous trivia question (if you have peeked at the answers already), *Planet of the Apes* is based on Pierre Boulle's 1963 French novel, *Monkey Planet* (*La Plante des Singes*). This was Messr. Boulle's first novel following the famous work, *Bridge on the River Kwai*. The novel is vastly different than the film. It begins with a young couple, Jinn and Phyllis, traveling through space when they receive a message from a journalist named Ulysee Merou. Merou is on an expedition with two other men (Professor Antelle and Arthur Levain) and a chimpanzee (Hector). The letter sent by Merou is a plea for help, because he and his companions have landed on a planet ruled by talking, intelligent apes. While on this planet, Merou becomes involved with and impregnates a mute female named Nova. Eventually, Merou, Nova, and their infant child are allowed to leave the planet and return home. When they land on Earth (Paris, France), however, they are greeted by a gorilla and we learn that Earth has been transformed into a planet ruled by apes. Further, we learn that Jinn and Phyllis are actually chimpanzees.

The novel also introduces an entirely different society than the one we see in the film. Messr. Boulle's simian society was a modern, twentieth century metropolis, where the apes drove automobiles and lived in big metropolitan cities. In fact, when the film was still seeking financial backing, the early pre-production concepts drawn up by William Creber, the film's art director, were done with a modern setting and technology. For example, the early pre-production drawing for the hunt scene involved the gorillas chasing and shooting the humans from helicopters and jeeps, not horses.[3]

Floating Through Space....

1. Do you know the first line spoken in *Planet of the Apes*?
2. What three things does Taylor do before going into the sleeping capsule?
3. What happens to the time clock when Taylor looks at it?
4. How does Taylor's physical appearance change after he awakes from his deep sleep?
5. What year is it on Earth while the astronauts are flying through space?
6. What year is it when they crash?
7. How long have the astronauts been traveling in space?
8. The spacecraft shows two different time periods on the clock. What are the names for the two time periods?

Abandon Ship

1. Where does the spacecraft land?
2. Where was the crash-landing scene filmed and what is the significance of this location?
3. What do the astronauts do when they realize the craft is sinking?
4. What color is the raft and what symbol appears on it?
5. How many astronauts are on the spacecraft?
6. Can you name all the astronauts on the spacecraft?
7. What happens to one of the astronauts?
8. How does Taylor say this occurred?
9. According to Taylor, how long was the astronaut in this state?
10. What three symbols appear on each astronaut's spacesuit?
11. How much time does Taylor say has passed on Earth?
12. After the crash, Taylor gives Dodge and Landon instructions. What are these instructions?
13. What are the results of the instructions given to Dodge and Landon?
14. What does Taylor say happened to the people who sent them on their mission?
15. What does Landon say as they are paddling away from the ship?
16. How does Taylor reply to Landon's remark?
17. From what location did the astronauts depart when they started their journey into space?
18. Where does Taylor say they are?
19. Do you know Taylor's full name?

Taylor contemplates man's destiny.

The astronauts abandon their spacecraft before it sinks and prepare to explore an unknown planet.

Better Than Man

What character made the following statement in *Planet of the Apes*?

I can't help thinking that somewhere in the universe there has to be something better than man, has to be.

Land Ho!

1. What test does Taylor have Dodge perform when they reach land?
2. What does Dodge conclude from this test?
3. Can you name all the supplies that Taylor describes that the astronauts are carrying in their backpacks?
4. Why do they only have 72 hours to find life on the planet?
5. Whose theory does Taylor say is true?
6. Do you know what symbol appears on the astronauts backpacks?
7. Taylor tells Landon he looks pretty chipper for someone who is how old?
8. What does Landon do before they begin their trek into the Forbidden Zone?
9. What is Taylor's reaction to this?

Script Approval

Who made the following statement regarding the script for *Planet of the Apes*?

Planet of the Apes was the only science-fiction script I'd seen with acting in it. I found it a very complicated plot with considerable social comment.[4]

The Forbidden Zone

1. How does Dodge explain the odd occurrences that transpire as the astronauts travel through the Forbidden Zone?

2. What object chases them as they are walking in the Forbidden Zone?
3. Where were the scenes of the astronauts trekking through the Forbidden Zone filmed?
4. When they stop for a break, how much water does Dodge say they have left?
5. Taylor tells Landon that Dodge would do something if he could learn something new. What would Dodge do?
6. What do the astronauts find in the Forbidden Zone that gives them hope there is life on the planet?
7. What nickname does Landon use when referring to Taylor?
8. What does Landon notice up on the hill?
9. What lures Taylor's attention away from the object on the hill?
10. How does Taylor react to the distraction on the hill?

Who am I????

"I was one of the world's foremost Shakespearean actors when I accepted the role as an intellectual ape in *Planet of the Apes*. My Broadway debut in 1935 was in *Romeo & Juliet*."[5] Who am I?

Human Life

1. As the astronauts are swimming, what does Landon notice?
2. What occurs as they are looking at this?
3. What happens to their clothes and supplies?
4. What are the mute humans doing while the astronauts watch them in the field?
5. Taylor makes a comment about the mute humans in the field. What was this comment?
6. How does Dodge react to this statement?
7. Landon makes a pessimistic remark following Dodge's statement. What does he say?
8. What assumption does Taylor make about the mute humans?

Taylor and Dodge scurry through the forest in *Planet of the Apes*.

Screen Test

Arthur Jacobs had a difficult time finding a company to finance the making of *Planet of the Apes*. In fact, he was turned down by almost every major motion picture company in his first effort to produce the film. At one point, Warner Brothers tentatively agreed to fund the film, but after a budget of over $7 million was prepared, they decided to pass on the project. If it were not for Arthur Jacobs perseverance, the film may have never been made. It took a five minute screen test with a budget of $7,455.00 to try and convince 20th Century-Fox that the concept would work on film. The screen test was written by Rod Serling, starred both Edward G. Robinson and Charlton Heston, and was directed by Franklin J. Schaffner.

The scene involved a conversation between Dr. Zaius and Thomas (changed to Taylor in the film) in a tent at an archeological dig site where a talking human doll was discovered. The scene also includes several storyboard drawings of different scenes that could be used for the proposed film. Although they thought the concept would work on film, 20th Century-Fox passed again. Shortly afterward, Arthur Jacobs started to follow the success of another science-fiction film, *Fantastic Voyage*. He eventually convinced Richard Zanuck that if *Fantastic Voyage* could be successful, then *Planet of the Apes* could be as well. Eventually, Richard Zanuck convinced the board at 20th Century-Fox to fund the film and he gave Arthur Jacobs the "green light" to begin filming the production.[6]

Edward G. Robinson portrays Dr. Zaius in the screen test for *Planet of the Apes*.

The Hunt

1. What causes the mute humans to start running?
2. Which type of ape is first shown?
3. What do the apes do to the humans during the hunt scene?
4. The apes use several methods to capture the humans. Can you name three?
5. What is Dodge's fate?
6. What happens to Landon?
7. How is Nova captured?
8. How does Taylor foil the apes' first attempt to catch him?
9. How is Taylor eventually caught?
10. What is the significance in the way Taylor is captured?

The gorilla soldiers prepare to fire on human prey during the hunt.

Special-Effect Tricks

Although they appear complex, the ape buildings were one of the easiest props to assemble for the film. They were constructed out of a polyurethane foam, which was shot out of a foam gun and settled in ten minutes. It also had the advantage of being much stronger, yet twenty times lighter, than plastic. You will also notice in the film that there are five buildings overlooking ape city on a hill. These were not made of the polyurethane foam, but were actually cardboard cut-outs of the ape dwellings.

Further, the cornfield used in the famous hunt scene took only six weeks to grow. The seven foot vegetation was grown from a fast growing species of maize, which allowed the filmmakers to have it ready in time for shooting. One other trick included a man-made pool and waterfall with artificial plumbing in which the astronauts swam. These are just a few of the special-effect tricks used during the filming for *Planet of the Apes*.[7]

Ape City

1. Where was Ape City constructed?
2. How do the gorilla soldiers celebrate the success of the hunt?
3. How are the dead human bodies displayed?
4. What is the first word spoken by an ape?
5. Who says it and when is it said?
6. How are the surviving humans transported back to Ape City?

Ape City!

Who is he????

This actor has been a film star since his pre-teens, and he deserted his New York photography studio to star in *Planet of the Apes*. He was first boosted to fame in *How Green Was My Valley*.[8] Who is he?

Caged Animals

1. After Taylor is captured, he is given a blood transfusion with Nova. Who performs the transfusion?
2. What is the name of the jail guard?
3. How does Dr. Galen react when Zira asks him if Taylor will survive?
4. How do the humans in the cage bathe?
5. What does Zira give the mute humans as a snack?
6. How does Julius respond to Zira's assertion that Taylor is trying to talk?
7. Why does Taylor try to draw Zira closer to him?
8. What is Dr. Zaius' reaction when Taylor tries to speak?
9. Who makes the following comment about Taylor:
   "He has a definite gift for mimicry."
10. Zira wonders how Taylor would score on a certain test. What is the name of this test?
11. Dr. Zaius was not in favor of performing certain studies on Taylor. What were these studies?
12. What does Dr. Zaius consider a question of "simian survival?"
13. While Taylor is being held in the cage, what present does Zira bring him?

Taylor attempts to show Dr. Zaius that he can understand him.

Who is she????

This actress won an Academy Award for her performance in *A Streetcar Named Desire*. She was born Janet Cole and played an animal psychologist in *Planet of the Apes*.[9] Who is she?

The Compound

1. How do Cornelius and Zira greet each other?
2. What is the first thing Cornelius asks Zira?
3. Who is referred to as "the young ape with a shovel" and who calls him this?
4. Why does Taylor get in a fight with one of the mute humans in the compound?
5. What does Taylor write in the sand?
6. How does Nova react to what is written?
7. Who makes the following statement and at whom is it directed:
   "As you dig for artifacts, be sure you don't bury your reputation."
8. How do the gorillas break up the fight in the cage between Taylor and the mute human?
9. According to Dr. Zaius, what does Zira think she can do with the humans?
10. After Dr. Zaius notices what Taylor wrote in the sand, how does he react?

Simian Survival

Where does the following passage appear?:
   Beware the beast man, for he is the devil's pawn. Alone among God's primates, he kills for sport, or lust, or greed. Yea, he will murder his brother to possess his brother's land. Let him not breed in great numbers, for he will make a desert of his home and yours. Shun him. Drive him back into his jungle lair: For he is the harbinger of death.

In the Cage

1. How does Taylor obtain Zira's pad and pen?
2. How does she retrieve them?
3. Why was Zira left alone with Taylor?
4. What does Taylor write on the pad?
5. How does Zira react to what is written?
6. What nickname does Zira give Taylor?

Ape Makeup

One of the greatest challenges in making *Planet of the Apes* was the creation of makeup that would be believable. The massive makeup process required the assistance of chemists, as well as makeup design artists, sculptors, and wigmakers. It had to present the ape characters as intelligent beings with makeup that would allow the actors' faces to be mobile. Makeup artist John Chambers described the first concept for the ape makeup as an Neanderthal type, where the character was fringing more on the human than the animal. He thought the makeup used in the screen test was crude, but it gave them an idea of what they wanted to do for the film. After a year of testing different makeup techniques and many hours spent transforming the actors and actresses from human to simian, it all paid off with some of the greatest makeup effects ever created.[10]

Maurice Evans, who portrayed the role of Dr. Zaius, revealed that the removal of the makeup was difficult on the skin. The makeup was applied with spirit gum, which has a great deal of highly concentrated alcohol as its base. This high alcohol content was very harsh to the skin. He further stated that the spirit gum set very hard and could only be removed with a combination of strong alcohol and acetone. He considered the removal of the makeup as the best part of the day because it took so long that he found himself inhaling the fumes, which would leave him with a buzz.[11]

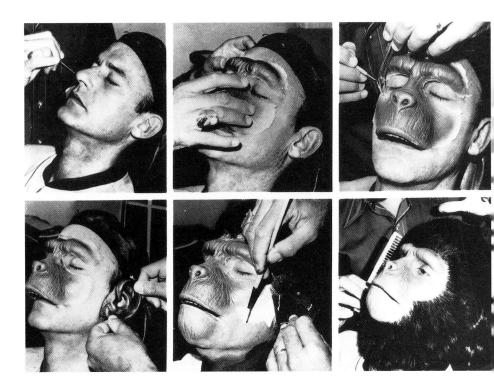

Roddy McDowall goes through the transformation from human to simian.

Cornelius' Office

1. What is the significance of Jefferson Public School?
2. Where was this learning institution located?
3. How does Taylor ask about Dodge and Landon?
4. What does Cornelius claim is an "scientific impossibility?"
5. How does Taylor demonstrate this impossibility?
6. Taylor asks Cornelius and Zira if they have something. What does he ask for?
7. How does Cornelius respond to Taylor's assertion that he traveled in the Forbidden Zone?
8. What theory did Cornelius formulate from his diggings in the Forbidden Zone?
9. Who arrives while Cornelius and Zira are communicating with Taylor?
10. Why did they arrive?
11. What is the rule about humans outside the compound?
12. How does Dr. Zaius react to the paper airplane?

Taylor tries to show Cornelius and Zira how he arrived on the planet.

Stewart

To achieve the corpse-like effect for Stewart's death, makeup artist John Chambers used a mold of Stewart over which he sculpted decomposing features on the head and originally used a mannequin for the body. Although he was happy with the head, he was unhappy with the way the body looked. Therefore, he auditioned elderly extras to find someone who had the right body. Eventually, he found an 83 year old woman who supplied the body effect he desired. The sequence was filmed with the "live" corpse with satisfying results.[12]

Taylor discovers a mummified Stewart after an air leak in her capsule killed her.

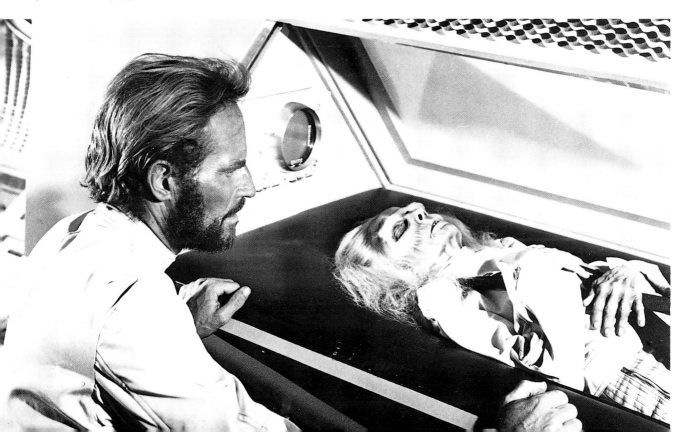

Matching Trivia

Match the following *Planet of the Apes* characters with the actor/actress who played them:

1. Dr. Zaius
2. Zira
3. Lucius
4. Dr. Galen
5. Dodge
6. Landon
7. Cornelius
8. Taylor
9. Hunt Leader
10. Nova
11. Julius
12. Dr. Maximus
13. Stewart
14. President of
    the Academy
15. Dr. Honorius
16. Minister

a. Roddy McDowall
b. Linda Harrison
c. Jeff Burton
d. Buck Kartalian
e. James Daly
f. Wright King
g. Maurice Evans
h. Woodrow Parfrey
i. James Whitmore
j. Robert Gunner
k. Paul Lambert
l. Norman Burton
m. Charlton Heston

n. Kim Hunter
o. Lou Wagner
p. Dianne Stanley

The Escape

1. The gorilla soldiers arrive at the cage and speak to Julius. Where does the lieutenant tell Julius they are taking Taylor?
2. How does Taylor escape?
3. What does Zira want Taylor and Nova to do?
4. After Taylor escapes, where is the first place he goes and what is taking place?
5. According to the Minister, what did the dear departed once say to him?
6. Who spots Taylor and what does he say?
7. At one point during his escape, Taylor is almost caught. How is he almost caught, and how does he get away again?
8. Who does Taylor find stuffed and on exhibit in the apes' Museum of Natural History?
9. After Taylor leaves the museum and runs outside, he is greeted by the citizens of Ape City. How do they greet him?
10. How is Taylor finally recaptured?
11. According to the security police, who is now in charge of Taylor?
12. What does Taylor say when the security policeman attempts to grab him?
13. How do the apes react to Taylor's ability to speak?

Lunchtime

When production first started on the film, it took six to seven hours to apply the ape makeup and three hours to remove it. Since time was important, new techniques had to be invented to speed up the application and removal of makeup. The makeup artists finally devised methods that took only two hours to apply, but the actors/actresses could not remove their makeup. Therefore, they had to wear their ape costumes all day. This created a problem at lunch time, when the actors and actresses had to use straws to eat their meals. Further, for some strange reason, all the gorillas sat together at one table, the chimpanzees at another, and the orangutans at another.[13]

Taylor's escape attempt fails as he is recaptured by the gorillas.

Back to the Cage

1. While the gorillas are removing Nova from the cage, how does Julius prevent Taylor from intervening?
2. What does Julius call Taylor?
3. How does Taylor reply to Julius' statement?
4. According to Taylor, who was Stewart going to be?
5. What does Taylor teach Nova to do?
6. Besides Julius, how many gorilla guards arrive to take Taylor from his cage?
7. Where do they take him?

What is the point?

When asked what he thought the point of *Planet of the Apes* was, Charlton Heston responded that "man is a seriously flawed animal, which must learn to deal with his flaws." Further, he thought *Planet of the Apes* could not only be published as a boy's book of adventure, but it could also be enjoyed as a fantastic adventure film.[14]

Ad Hoc Tribunal of the National Academy

1. How many apes are on the Tribunal and what type of ape are they?
2. Can you name the apes on the Tribunal?
3. Taylor is not allowed to do something in court. What is he not allowed to do?
4. Who represents the state?
5. What rights does Taylor have under "ape law?"
6. What does Dr. Zaius say they are doing with Taylor?
7. What are the ramifications when Taylor speaks in court?
8. What is the following?

> That the almighty created the ape in his own image; that he gave him a soul and a mind; that he set him apart from the beasts of the jungle and made him the lord of the planet.

9. Why was Taylor really brought to court?
10. The bailiff was given specific instructions prior to the hearing. What were these instructions?
11. What does the President of the Academy tell Dr. Honorius not to do?
12. Honorius tests Taylor's reasoning by asking him several questions. How many of these questions do you know?
13. How does Taylor respond to these questions?
14. Taylor gives Cornelius a note to read to the Tribunal. What does the note say?
15. A last ditch effort is made to prove Taylor's innocence. What happens?
16. Who is Taylor looking for in the round-up?
17. What provokes Taylor to call Dr. Zaius a "bloody baboon?"
18. When they get back into court, how does Dr. Zaius explain what happened to Landon?
19. How does Cornelius come to Taylor's defense?
20. What did Cornelius discover in the Forbidden Zone?
21. Who is Cornelius referring to when he says the following:

> Behold this marvel, this living paradox, this missing link in an evolutionary chain.

22. Why was Cornelius' travel permit canceled?
23. What are the charges against Cornelius and Zira?
24. Under what circumstances does the following take place and who articulates this:

> Hear no evil, See no evil, Speak no evil.

Taylor is led into court to face the tribunal.

Taylor is tried before the ad hoc Tribunal of the National Academy.

Taylor discovers Landon's fate on the *Planet of the Apes*.

More Matching Trivia

Match the following characters to the position or relationship they hold on the *Planet of the Apes*: (Answers may be used more than once)

1. Cornelius
2. Zira
3. Dr. Zaius
4. Taylor
5. Julius
6. Lucius
7. Dr. Honorius
8. Marcus
9. Stewart
10. Nova
11. Dr. Galen
12. Dodge
13. Dr. Maximus

a. Commissioner for Animal Affairs
b. Skipper
c. Zira's Nephew
d. Medical Doctor
e. Deputy Minister of Justice
f. Afro-American Astronaut
g. Jail Guard
h. Female Astronaut
i. Bright Eyes
j. Minister of Science
k. Archeologist
l. Head of Security
m. Animal Psychologist
n. Mute Female
o. Chief Defender of Faith

Cornelius

As you know from a previous trivia question, Roddy McDowall played the role of Cornelius, but do you know how he actually came to be involved with the film? Well, Arthur Jacobs approached him regarding the part of Cornelius a year before production started. He was one of the few people that Mr. Jacobs explained the whole story to, including the ending. The character of Cornelius was described to him and Mr. McDowall thought he was very intriguing. A year later he signed on to be part of the film and have his face molded for the makeup. He also thought the first film was very difficult because it was made in the summertime and with all the quartz lights the temperature felt like 140 degrees.[15]

Dr. Zaius' Office

1. The tribunal has placed Taylor in Dr. Zaius' custody for final disposition. What does Dr. Zaius plan on doing with Taylor, if he doesn't tell him where his tribe is located?
2. What does Dr. Zaius have the power to give Taylor if he tells him where his tribe is located?
3. Why does Taylor thank Dr. Zaius?
4. What does Dr. Zaius want Taylor to tell him, in order to save himself?
5. How does Dr. Zaius refer to Taylor at the end of their conversation?
6. How long does Dr. Zaius give Taylor to make a full confession?
7. What method does Dr. Zaius plan on using to obtain the information he is seeking from Taylor?
8. Why does Dr. Zaius fear Taylor?
9. What are the Sacred Scrolls?
10. Who wrote the Sacred Scrolls?

Taylor is summoned by Dr. Zaius for his final disposition.

Dr. Zira

When asked what her initial approach was for the Zira character after she read the script for *Planet of the Apes*, Kim Hunter said Zira "came through strongly as a person and that she never saw her as an ape." She also thought John Chambers' makeup helped her achieve the transformation into the ape-woman quite amazingly, or, as in her words, "the makeup achievements were larger than life."[16]

Zira's Plan

1. What is Julius doing when Lucius comes to the jail?
2. Who is Lucius?
3. According to Lucius, what organization wants to save Taylor from "the butchers in the lab?"
4. Where does Lucius say he is from?
5. What does Julius want to see, before he will release Taylor?
6. Where does Lucius say they are transferring the beast?
7. What is wrong with the document that Lucius gives Julius?
8. What is the real reason Lucius has come to the jail?
9. How does Lucius help Taylor escape?
10. After he is released from his cage, Taylor insists on bringing something with him. What does he want to bring with him?

George Taylor, Jr.????

In the original script for *Planet of the Apes*, written by Rod Serling, Nova becomes pregnant with Taylor's child. Taylor is killed by a gorilla sniper and Nova escapes into the Forbidden Zone. The point with this ending was if Nova gives birth to a boy and he grows to manhood, then the species will survive. If not, man becomes extinct. This would have left open the door for a sequel. The idea of Nova being pregnant was deleted at the insistence of a high ranking official at 20th Century-Fox who found it distasteful.[17]

Back to the Forbidden Zone

1. Taylor complains that the clothes Zira gave him stink. How does Lucius respond to Taylor's griping?
2. What is their plan in case they are stopped by the gorilla soldiers?
3. After they are a safe distance from Ape City, who meets them?
4. What is the first thing Taylor asks for after they let him out of the wagon?
5. Why are Cornelius and Zira on the run?
6. Where do Cornelius and Zira plan on going?
7. How long does Cornelius say it will take them to reach there destination?
8. When Cornelius asks Taylor what they will find at Dead Lake, how does he respond?
9. Where does Cornelius tell Taylor the river leads?
10. According to Cornelius, why do they call it the Forbidden Zone?
11. Who is the greatest ape of all?

Taylor, Nova, Zira, and Cornelius take a break in the Forbidden Zone.

Surprise Ending

The ending to *Planet of the Apes* was so secret that people on the set weren't even suppose to know how the film was going to end. When all the advertising publicity was being distributed prior to its release, none of the advertising disclosed how the film would end. In fact, the following disclaimer appeared at the end of the summary for the film:

> (*Note*: The shocking conclusion of *Planet of the Apes* will not be revealed in any synopsis.)[18]

Archeological Diggings

1. What does Taylor do when they get to the dig sight that causes Cornelius to tell him he looks less intelligent?
2. Who says he doesn't go in for fads, after Taylor tells him only kids wore beards?
3. When they start going up to the cave, something happens. What happens and who notices it?
4. What does Dr. Zaius say as he approaches?
5. Who does Dr. Zaius call an "apostate" & "fool" and why does he call him this?
6. Why does Taylor make the following comment?
   "On this planet it's easy."
7. When were the Sacred Scrolls written?
8. What does Taylor propose to Dr. Zaius?

Dr. Zaius and the gorilla soldiers track Taylor down in the Forbidden Zone.

The Good Dr. Zaius

When asked what he saw in Dr. Zaius' character, Maurice Evans made the following assessment in an 1972 interview in *Cinefantastique* magazine:

> He is the chief minister of Science in the ape world; in addition, he's the keeper of the scrolls, a kind of Moses of the ape civilization. He has a knowledge and wisdom which is denied other people. He has interpreted the ape scriptures in such a way that he feels he has a greater knowledge of what has gone before and what is likely to follow. His main concern is to ensure that the ape civilization is not challenged, by any other civilization. He wants to retain the status quo, so he is trying to discourage the younger apes—the chimpanzees—who are making scientific experiments on the subhuman characters that are the other occupants of the planet—which involve operations on their brains to keep them subjugated and inferior—he discourages them from interpreting these experiments. He sees danger with too little knowledge.[19]

On a personal note, I wanted to mention that Dr. Zaius is my favorite character from *Planet of the Apes*. He is an intelligent character, whose part was very well-written. He carries himself with a great deal of dignity and protects the apes' civilization from the truth of their past. I also think he has some great quotes in the film, which you will notice throughout this trivia section.

Maurice Evans portrays Dr. Zaius.

The Cave

1. Can you name everyone who explores the cave?
2. Who is not allowed to go to the cave and why?
3. What is "the paradox?"
4. What does Zira tell Cornelius to show them?
5. How does Dr. Zaius respond to this finding?
6. Where does the following passage appear:
   > "And Proteus brought the upright beast into the garden, and chained him to a tree, and the children did make sport of him."
7. Name the three items in the cave that Taylor observes?
8. What is the conclusive evidence they find in the cave that proves man was on the planet before the ape?
9. What does this evidence do that proves this?
10. What question does Taylor ask Dr. Zaius when they find this evidence?
11. What draws their attention from the cave?

A Tough Shoot

According to Charlton Heston, the shooting of *Planet of the Apes* proved to be a tough one. To begin with, in an effort to keep the budget down on a film that was testing uncharted waters, Fox had cut ten days off the shooting schedule. Production on the film began on May 21, 1967, and got off on the wrong foot when the beards for Dodge and Landon were not sent to the set (neither of the actors had time to grow their own). When they did arrive, they weren't applied well, causing a delay in shooting on day one. The heat was also unbearable, causing one of the astronauts to pass out from it.

Also during the production, Charlton Heston got a terrible cold that reduced his voice to a hoarse rasp. The following day he had one line of dialogue, which ironically was one of most famous lines in the film. Following his capture after he escapes, Taylor says, "Take your stinking paws off me you damn dirty ape!" It turned out to be the exact voice needed for the scene.[20]

Climactic Conclusion

1. What did the gorilla soldiers do with all the supplies?
2. How did the gorilla soldiers get the supplies?
3. How does Taylor trick Dr. Zaius into coming out of the cave?
4. What does Taylor say to lure Dr. Zaius from the cave?
5. Cornelius says the gorilla soldiers took everything, but Taylor says they left something. What is he referring to?
6. Taylor gives Lucius instructions. What are these instructions?
7. What does Taylor threaten to do if he doesn't get the supplies?
8. How was Taylor humiliated by the apes?
9. What does Taylor do to Dr. Zaius?
10. Why does Taylor say humans did not survive?

Taylor lures Dr. Zaius from the cave and takes him hostage.

Man

Who makes the following statement, to whom is it made and why?:
> Because you're a man. And you're right, I have always known about man. From the evidence, I believe his wisdom must walk hand in hand with his idiocy. His emotions must rule his brain. He must be a warlike creature who gives battle to everything around him, even himself.

Talking Doll

Did you know that the talking doll was used twice in the production of *Planet of the Apes*? Besides being used in the finished film, Arthur Jacobs also utilized it when he made the five minute screen test to convince 20th Century-Fox to fund the film. This simple talking prop played an important role in the film, because it proved that man was on Earth prior to the ape.

Conclusion Continued....

11. Why did Dr. Zaius fear man's coming?
12. Where does Taylor say he will go?
13. Under what circumstances does Cornelius say the following:
    > His culture is our culture.
14. How does Taylor say good-bye to Zira?
15. What does Taylor advise Lucius to "keep flying?"
16. What does Zira say when Taylor asks her if he can kiss her good-bye?
17. What did Dr. Zaius mean by the following phrase?:
    > Don't look for it Taylor, you may not like what you find.
18. What specific instructions does Dr. Zaius give the gorillas?
19. Why does he give these specific instructions?
20. What was Dr. Zaius referring to when he made the following statement:
    > I may just have saved it for you.
21. How does Dr. Zaius respond to Zira's question as to what Taylor will find in the Forbidden Zone?

22. What does Taylor discover in the Forbidden Zone along the shore-line?
23. What is the significance of this discovery?
24. How does he respond to what he has found?
25. Do you know the significance that Point Dune, California plays in *Planet of the Apes*?

Taylor and Nova ride off into the Forbidden Zone in search of man's destiny.

Dr. Zaius is held captive by Taylor.

The Classic Ending

Since Pierre Boulle's ending from the novel was not used in the film, where do you think the idea for one of the most climactic endings in movie history originated. The following quote from Arthur Jacobs describes the birth of the Statue of Liberty scene:

> I was having lunch at the Yugo Kosherama Deli-catessen in Burbank, across the street from Warner Brothers and was saying to Blake Edwards (who was originally slated to direct the film) 'What if he was on the Earth the whole time and doesn't know it?' And as we walked out, after paying for the two ham sand-wiches, we looked up and there was this big Statue of Liberty on the wall of the delicatessen. We both looked at each other and said, 'Rosebud.' If we'd never had lunch in that delicatessen, I doubt that we would have had the Statue of Liberty as the end of the picture.[21]

It's not the New York Times!

1. As a bonus, can you name the newspaper that was given away at movie theaters and in the press kit during the release of *Planet of the Apes*?
2. For an extra bonus, do you know what the headlines for this newspaper read?

Crate of What????

After Arthur Jacobs read Rod Serling's original script for *Planet of the Apes*, he told him that he would win an Oscar for it. Rod Serling responded by asking for a crate of bananas, so Arthur Jacobs obliged by giving him four crates of them.[22] Do you think this really happened?

A Day at the Beach

The climactic conclusion of *Planet of the Apes* was filmed at Point Dune, California, a remote segment of California sea-coast between Malibu and Oxnard. The area has 130-foot cliffs towering above the shoreline and there were no roads or trails leading down to the shooting area. Therefore, the cast, crew, equipment, and horses had to be lowered onto the sand in a huge bucket suspended from a giant crane.[23]

Charlton Heston
in
An Arthur P. Jacobs Production

Planet Of The Apes

Cast

George Taylor	Charlton Heston
Cornelius	Roddy McDowall
Zira	Kim Hunter
Dr. Zaius	Maurice Evans
President of the Academy	James Whitmore
Honorius	James Daly
Nova	Linda Harrison
Landon	Robert Gunner
Lucius	Lou Wagner

Maximus	Woodrow Parfrey
Dodge	Jeff Burton
Julius	Buck Kartalian
Hunt Leader	Norman Burton
Dr. Galen	Wright King
Minister	Paul Lambert
Produced by	Arthur P. Jacobs
Directed by	Franklin J. Schaffner
Associate Producer	Mort Abrahams
Screenplay by	Michael Wilson & Rod Serling
Based on the novel by	Pierre Boulle
Music by	Jerry Goldsmith
Creative Makeup Design	John Chambers
Directory of Photography	Leon Shamroy, A.S.C.
Art Direction	Jack Martin Smith
	William Creber
Set Decorations	Walter M. Scott
	Norman Rockett
Special Photographic Effects	L.B. Abbott, A.S.C.
	Art Cruickshank
	Emil Kosa, Jr.
Film Editor	Hugh S. Fowler, A.C.E.
Unit Production Manager	William Eckardt
Assistant Director	William Kissel
Sound	Herman Lewis
	David Dockendorf
Costumes Designed by	Morton Haack
Makeup by	Ben Nye
	Dan Striepeke, S.M.A.
Hairstyling by	Edith Lindon
Orchestration	Arthur Morton
Filmed in PANAVISION ®	Color in DELUXE

Produced by APJAC Productions, Inc.
and Released by Twentieth Century-Fox Film Corporation

Answer Key to Planet of the Apes *Trivia*

Background Trivia

1. *Beneath the Planet of the Apes.*
2. David Watson.
3. She did not appear in *Planet of the Apes.*
4. Hollywood columnist James Bacon and Variety columnist Army Archerd appeared in all five ape films. Arthur Jacobs gave bit parts to columnists to get p.r. for the films.
5. *Monkey Planet.*
6. Pierre Boulle.
7. *Bridge on the River Kwai.*
8. John Chambers.
9. Jerry Goldsmith.
10. Michael Wilson and Rod Serling.
11. Marlon Brando, Paul Newman, and Burt Lancaster.
12. Edward G. Robinson.
13. Maurice Evans.
14. Arthur Jacobs.
15. By first putting together a five minute screen test to prove the makeup would work, and then monitoring the success of another science-fiction film, *Fantastic Voyage,* to prove that if this film could be successful, then *Planet of the Apes* could.
16. Richard Zanuck.
17. Edward G. Robinson, Charlton Heston, James Brolin, and Linda Harrison.
18. Dr. Zaius, Thomas (later changed to Taylor), Cornelius, and Zira.
19. Franklin J. Schaffner.
20. Arthur P. Jacobs.
21. Orangutan, Chimpanzee, and Gorilla.
22. Orangutans are the administrators, chimpanzees are the scientists, and gorillas are the soldiers.
23. Gorillas.
24. Baboons.
25. They were going to be the lowest class, below gorillas.
26. Thomas.
27. *The Hunt.*
28. Morton Haack was nominated for costume design.
29. Tim Daly, James Daly, and Dr. Honorius.
30. "*Planet of the Apes*, beyond your wildest dreams."
31. Leon Shamroy, A.S.C.

Astronaut George Taylor.

An early pre-production drawing of a gorilla soldier.

An early pre-production drawing of a male chimpanzee.

An early pre-production drawing of a female chimpanzee.

Floating Through Space....

1. "And that completes my final report until we reach touchdown."
2. Records a message, smokes a cigar, and gives himself a shot.
3. It changes from 3/26/2673 to 3/27/2673.
4. He has grown a beard.
5. July 14, 1972.
6. November 25, 3978.
7. Eighteen calendar months, but some 2,000 years in terms of the mathematics of time and space.
8. Earth Time and Space Time.

Abandon Ship

1. In a lake within the Forbidden Zone.
2. Lake Powell, Utah, on the Colorado River in four hundred feet deep water. This location was a top government security area and it was the first time a film company was ever allowed to film in the region.
3. Abandon ship.
4. Yellow with an American flag.
5. Four.
6. Taylor, Landon, Dodge, and Stewart.
7. Stewart dies in her sleep.
8. An air leak in her sleep capsule.
9. Over a year.
10. American flag, ANSA patch, and a patch with their name on it.
11. 700 years.
12. He tells Dodge to check the atmosphere and Landon to send out a signal to Earth that they have landed.
13. Dodge says the air is fine and Landon can't send out a signal because there is no power.
14. "They've long since come and gone."
15. "She's sinking. Going, going, gone."
16. He says, "Okay, we're here to stay."
17. Cape Kennedy.
18. "We're some 320 light years from Earth on an unnamed planet in orbit around a star on the constellation of Orion."
19. Commander George Taylor.

An early pre-production drawing of Ape City.

An early pre-production drawing of the Animal Lab.

Better Than Man

George Taylor.

Land Ho!

1. Soil Test.
2. "Nothing will grow here, there's a trace of carbohydrates, all of the nitrogen is locked into the nitrates."
3. One pistol, 20 rounds of ammunition, medical kit, TX9, camera, food and water. Dodge is carrying the sensors and Geiger counter.
4. That's when the "groceries" (food & water) run out.
5. Dr. Victor Hasselin's theory.
6. The American flag.
7. 2,031 years old.
8. He plants a small American flag in the ground.
9. He laughs hysterically.

Script Approval

Charlton Heston.

An early pre-production drawing of the hunt scene.

The Forbidden Zone

1. "It doesn't add up, thunder and lightning, and no rain. Cloud covered night and that strange luminosity, yet there's no moon."
2. Boulders.
3. Wilderness area around Lake Powell on the Colorado River in Utah and Arizona.
4. Eight ounces.
5. He would walk naked into a live volcano.
6. A small plant.
7. Skipper.
8. Scarecrows.
9. A waterfall and pond.
10. He says, "To hell with the scarecrows."

Who am I????

Maurice Evans.

Human Life

1. Footprints in the mud.
2. Their clothes are stolen by the mute humans.
3. The clothes are ripped apart and supplies are thrown all over the ground.
4. They are eating fruit and corn.
5. "Well, at least they haven't tried to bite us yet."
6. "Blessed thou the vegetarians."
7. "We got off at the wrong stop."
8. "You're suppose to be the optimist, Landon; look on the bright side, if this is the best they've got around here, in six months we'll be running this planet."

The Hunt

1. A loud horn.
2. Gorillas.
3. The gorillas pursue, capture, and/or kill the humans.
4. Guns, rope, nets, clubs, and long sticks.
5. He is shot in the back of neck and killed.
6. He is hit in the face and knocked out.
7. The gorillas capture her in a net.
8. The gorillas' net gets caught on a tree stump that Taylor jumps over and they are thrown from their horses.
9. He is shot in the throat and falls off a small cliff into a gully.
10. He is unable to speak.

Ape City

1. It was constructed on the 20th Century-Fox ranch in the San Fernando Valley.
2. Three of them have their picture taken with the dead bodies.
3. They are either hung upside down or piled in a stack.
4. "Smile."
5. A gorilla says this as he is taking a picture of the three gorillas posing with the dead humans.
6. In a caged wagon.

Who is he??

Roddy McDowall.

Caged Animals

1. Dr. Galen.
2. Julius.
3. "I don't know, this beast has lost a lot of blood."
4. They are sprayed with a hose.
5. Sugar cubes.
6. "You know what they say, human see, human do."
7. So he can grab her pad and pen.
8. He says, "A man acting like an ape." He goes on further to say that man has no understanding and can only be taught a few simple tricks.
9. Dr. Zaius.
10. Hopkins Manual Dexterity Test.
11. Behavioral Studies.
12. That the sooner Taylor is exterminated the better.
13. Nova.

Dr. Galen and his assistant work to save Taylor's life after he is shot during the hunt. Dr. Zira observes the procedure.

A human runs for his life as the gorilla soldiers pursue him during the hunt.

Dr. Zaius discusses Taylor's actions with Zira.

Dr. Zaius holds the paper airplane that Taylor made to show how he landed on the planet.

Who is she????
Kim Hunter.

The Compound
1. They kiss.
2. "Do you have to work tonight?"
3. Cornelius by Dr. Zaius.
4. The mute human tries to erase what Taylor writes in the sand.
5. I can write.
6. She erases part of what Taylor wrote.
7. Dr. Zaius says it to Cornelius.
8. With a burning torch and whip.
9. She thinks man can be domesticated.
10. He erases the "wri" that Taylor wrote in the sand with his cane.

Simian Survival
The Sacred Scrolls, 29th scroll, 6th verse.

In the Cage
1. He grabs her when she gets too close to the cage.
2. Julius goes into the cage and retrieves them for her.
3. Julius went to get ointment for Taylor's burn.
4. My name is Taylor.
5. She tells Julius to get a collar and leash, because she is taking him out of the cage.
6. Bright eyes.

Cornelius' Office
1. This is where Taylor was educated.
2. Fort Wayne, Indiana.
3. He writes on a piece of paper, "Dodge was killed in the hunt. What happened to Landon?"
4. Flight.
5. By making and tossing a paper airplane into the air.
6. Maps.
7. He says "Out of the question. No creature can survive in the Forbidden Zone. I know. I've been there."
8. That ape evolved from a lower order of primate, possibly man.
9. Dr. Zaius, Dr. Maximus, and two gorillas.
10. Cornelius was suppose to meet with Dr. Zaius, but he was late.
11. No animals are allowed outside the compound, especially without a leash.
12. Crumbles it up and drops it on the ground.

Taylor discovers a stuffed Dodge in the Apes museum.

Matching Trivia

1. g.	9. l.
2. n.	10. b.
3. o.	11. d.
4. f.	12. h.
5. c.	13. p.
6. j.	14. i.
7. a.	15. e.
8. m.	16. k.

The Escape

1. To the vet to have him gelded.
2. He grabs Julius when he tries to put a lease on him and knocks him out.
3. Mate.
4. He runs into a building, where a funeral is taking place.
5. "I never met an ape I didn't like."
6. A young gorilla child who says, "Look, it's a man."
7. A gorilla gets a lease around Taylor's neck, but he able to free himself and knock the gorilla off the roof of the building.
8. Dodge.
9. They throw rocks, fruit, and vegetables at him. Of course, they were actually *rubber* rocks, fruit, and vegetables!
10. The gorillas drop a net on him and pull it up.
11. The Ministry of Science.
12. "Take your stinking paws off me you damn dirty ape!"
13. They are shocked, because they thought man was incapable of speaking.

Taylor is pelted with rocks, fruit, and vegetables by the citizens of Ape City.

Back to the Cage

1. By spraying him with a hose.
2. A freak.
3. He says, "It's a madhouse, a madhouse."
4. The new Eve.
5. Smile.
6. Three.
7. To the courtroom.

The gorilla soldiers converge on Taylor during his escape attempt.

Taylor is led back to the cage by a pair of gorilla soldiers as Nova anticipates his return.

Ad Hoc Tribunal of the National Academy

1. Three, Orangutans.
2. Dr. Zaius, Dr. Maximus, and the President of the Academy.
3. Speak.
4. Dr. Honorius.
5. He has no rights under ape law.
6. That Taylor is not being tried, he is being disposed of.
7. The first time they tighten his lease. The second time they gag him.
8. First article of faith.
9. To expose Cornelius and Zira.
10. To clean-up the beast, because his rags gave off a stench that was offensive to the Tribunal.
11. Not to turn the hearing into a farce.
12. What is second article of faith? Why are all apes created equal? Why do men have no soul? What is the proof that a divine spark exists in the simian brain?
13. He admits he is not familiar with the ape culture.
14. "I have come to you from a planet in a different solar system. I am an explorer in space."
15. They assemble the remaining, surviving humans in the amphitheater that were captured in the hunt.
16. Landon.
17. He realizes they have given Landon a lobotomy.
18. He says, "The human specimen you saw outside suffered a skull fracture. Two fine veterinary surgeons, under my direction, were able to save his life."
19. That Taylor comes from somewhere in the Forbidden Zone, because Cornelius had been there, and Taylor described it accurately.
20. He discovered evidence of a simian culture that existed long before the Sacred Scrolls were written.
21. Taylor.
22. According to Dr. Zaius, he exceeded his orders.
23. They are indicted on contempt of tribunal, malicious mischief, and scientific heresy.
24. The ape tribunal (Dr. Zaius, Dr. Maximus, President of the Academy) do this when Zira and Cornelius are speaking out loud regarding Taylor's innocence.

Taylor is restrained by two gorillas for speaking during the tribunal.

A net is thrown over Taylor after he attempts to attack Dr. Zaius following the discovery of Landon's fate.

The President of the Academy makes a point during the tribunal, while Dr. Zaius observes the action.

A gorilla soldier towers over Taylor.

More Matching Trivia

1. k.	8. l.
2. m.	9. h.
3. j. and o.	10. n.
4. b. and i.	11. d.
5. g.	12. f.
6. c.	13. a.
7. e.	
8. l.	

Dr. Zaius' Office

1. "Emasculation to begin with, then experimental surgery. On the speech centers, on the brain. Eventually, a kind of living death."
2. A reprieve.
3. Dr. Zaius calls him Taylor.
4. If there is another jungle beyond the Forbidden Zone.
5. He calls him a menace and a walking pestilence.
6. Six hours.
7. He will use surgery to obtain it.
8. Because man is destructive and Taylor is a man.
9. The apes religious scriptures.
10. They were written by the Lawgiver.

Zira's Plan

1. He is smoking a cigar.
2. Zira's nephew.
3. Anti-vivisectionist society.
4. Office of Animal Affairs.
5. The order.
6. To the zoo.
7. It needs to be countersigned by Dr. Zaius.
8. To help Taylor escape.
9. He pushes Julius against the cage, Taylor grabs him and Lucius knocks him over the head with a club.
10. Nova.

See no evil. Hear no evil. Speak no evil.

Taylor and Nova are held on leashes by a gorilla soldier with a statue of the Lawgiver in the background. This scene did not appear in the film.

Back to the Forbidden Zone

1. "What do you expect, an ape's new suit?"
2. They are going to tell them they are taking Taylor to the zoo.
3. Cornelius.
4. If they have any weapons.
5. They have been indicted on heresy charges.
6. Back to the diggings in the Forbidden Zone that Cornelius made the year before.
7. "It is a three day ride across the desert."
8. "An empty rubber life raft, maybe a little flag."
9. To a sea some miles away, near the diggings Cornelius previously worked on.
10. "No one knows, it's an ancient taboo set forth in the Sacred Scrolls. The Lawgiver pronounced this whole area deadly."
11. The Lawgiver.

Archeological Diggings

1. He shaves off his beard.
2. Lucius.
3. Dr. Zaius arrives with the gorillas. Zira notices their arrival.
4. "You are all under arrest."
5. He says this to Cornelius, because according to Dr. Zaius, "only an apostate would flee to the Forbidden Zone and only a fool would give a gun to an animal."
6. When Dr. Zaius says he was surprised that man could be monogamous.
7. 1,200 years ago.
8. If they can prove that the Scared Scrolls don't tell the whole truth of the apes' history. If they can find some real evidence of another culture from some remote past, will he let them go?

Taylor, Nova, Cornelius, Zira, and Lucius travel through the Forbidden Zone en route to the dig site.

Taylor takes aim at Dr. Zaius, as Cornelius, Nova, and Lucius look on.

The Cave

1. Taylor, Nova, Cornelius, Zira, and Dr. Zaius.
2. Lucius, because he has to guard the horses and supplies.
3. The more ancient culture is the more advanced.
4. The human doll.
5. He says his granddaughter plays with human dolls.
6. The 13th Scroll in the Sacred Scrolls.
7. Eye glasses, false teeth, and a pre-fabricated heart valve.
8. The human doll can speak.
9. It says, "Mamma."
10. "Would an ape make a human doll that talks?"
11. They hear a gunshot.

Climactic Conclusion

1. They stole all the supplies (food and water).
2. They snuck up on Lucius while he was feeding the horses.
3. He pretends he was shot.
4. "Cornelius, Zira, help me."
5. They left a hostage behind, Dr. Zaius.
6. He tells him to go around the rocks and tell the gorillas they are holding Dr. Zaius hostage. They want a horse, food and water for a week, and 50 rounds of ammunition.
7. He will kill Dr. Zaius.
8. They led him around on a leash.
9. He ties him up to a tree stump.
10. "Wiped out by a plague, some natural catastrophe. A storm of meteors by the looks of some parts of this planet."

The greatest ape of all and author of the Sacred Scrolls, the Lawgiver.

Man

Dr. Zaius makes this statement to Taylor after Taylor asks him why he fears and hates him.

Conclusion Continued....

11. Because the Forbidden Zone was once a paradise, and Taylor's breed made a desert out of it.
12. He is going to follow the shoreline and his nose.
13. This is how Cornelius responds to Taylor when Taylor asks Cornelius and Zira to come with him. Cornelius responds that they can't go with him, because Dr. Zaius' culture is their culture.
14. He gives her a kiss on the lips.
15. The flags of discontent.
16. "All right, but you're so damned ugly."
17. Taylor says there's got to be a reason for what happened to the Forbidden Zone.

18. To fetch the dynamite, so they can seal up the cave.
19. So the evidence (talking doll) is buried and there will be no evidence that man was on the planet before the apes.
20. This was Dr. Zaius' response when Lucius asks him about the future.
21. "His destiny!"
22. The Statue of Liberty half buried in the sand.
23. He realizes he has been on Earth the whole time and that humans have finally had the long feared nuclear war that would blow away civilization.
24. He falls to his knees and says, "Oh my God. I'm back. I'm home. All the time it was, we finally really did it! You maniacs! You blew it up! Oh, damn you! God damn you all to hell!"
25. This is where the Statue of Liberty scene was filmed.

Taylor discovers a half-buried Statue of Liberty in the shocking conclusion to *Planet of the Apes.*

Dr. Zaius talks to Cornelius, while Zira, Marcus, and Lucius watch.

It's not the *New York Times*!

1. *The Ape.*
2. Latest Hunt a Great Success, Big Round-up of Human Beasts.

Crate of What????

Yes, this is how Rod Serling responded to Arthur Jacob's intuition about being nominated for an Academy Award.

The Sacred Scrolls
A Guide to Planet of the Apes Collectibles and Memorabilia

The intention of this price guide is to provide accurate information on collectibles and memorabilia from the *Planet of the Apes* films, television series, and animated cartoon. My purpose is to provide a list of as many *Planet of the Apes* items as possible along with an approximate price range for these items. For me, it's like reliving my childhood. I can remember going to our local Two Guys department store and heading straight to the toy department. There I would find shelves full of *Planet of the Apes* merchandise. I can remember it like it was yesterday. When I started re-collecting ape merchandise, I searched my attic in the hope of finding some of the old ape toys from my childhood. To my surprise and delight, I was able to salvage a Dr. Zaius Mego figure, Galen bank, General Ursus model kit, General Aldo box puzzle, and remnants of the board game. None of these items are in mint condition, but they hold a special meaning for me, as they are the original toys I played with two decades ago.

Most of the merchandise was released in 1973 and 1974, so you will not be able to enter your local toy store to purchase these items today. I have found the following areas the most fruitful in my never-ending search for ape memorabilia: toy shows, flea markets, garage sales, and publications such as *Toy Shop* — a bi-weekly circulation which provides listings for thousands of toys being sold by people like you and me. Via *Toy Shop* I have been able to find a majority of my collection and it has proven a successful source for *Planet of the Apes* contacts. There are approximately 20 to 25 additional ape collectors and dealers throughout the country with whom I buy, sell, trade, and exchange information regarding ape collectibles.

In the course of the past four years I have put together a collection of over 400 pieces of memorabilia from *Planet of the Apes*, including both toys and paper products. One of my most cherished pieces is the one sheet movie poster from the original *Planet of the Apes*. This piece is literally impossible to find rolled, but you can find folded versions in near mint condition. Another important part of my collection includes Don Post masks of Cornelius (1st Series), Dr. Zaius (2nd Series), and General Aldo (2nd Series). The First Series was released in 1974 and the Second Series was released in 1983. These items are not considered rare and can be located in various conditions with some time and effort. One of the items which is hard to find in mint condition is the set of eight 11"x14" lobby cards from the first film. This is another item that can be found with time, although it is difficult to find in mint condition. Prices for these items can be found in their respective sections of the guide.

A majority of the listed merchandise is considered "common" and can be located with a little time. There are a number of items, however, which are considered "rare." These items are more difficult to locate. Once located, you will have to pay premium price for them. One of the most challenging items to find is the British ring set. This set consists of small plastic rings, made by Stan Lee Company, which contain small pic-

tures of various ape's heads. A set of these rings, when located, can command a price of up to $2,000. When sold individually, one could expect to pay as much as $400 each. Another troublesome item is the door panel posters released in conjunction with the first film. The set of four door panels can be sold for as much as $1,500 and $250-300 for one, but they are extremely difficult to locate. These are only a few examples of some of the rare ape items.

The easiest way to differentiate between the licensed and unlicensed items is to look for the APJAC logo. This was the production company started by Arthur Jacobs when the first *Planet of the Apes* film was made. The APJAC logo appears somewhere on both the packaging and the product for all of the items that were licensed. For example, on the Mego figures, the word APJAC appears in small letters on the back of the figure's head. It should also be noted that the logo will show the date of 1967. Although the year 1967 is listed, this was not the year the product was actually produced. The 1967 date was the year that 20th Century-Fox copyrighted APJAC Productions making of *Planet of the Apes*.

The majority of *Planet of the Apes* merchandise was released during 1973-1974 in association with the release of the *Go Ape* movie festival and the television series. The only merchandise released in 1968, in conjunction with the release of the first film, was the Topps set of 44 trading cards and the movie soundtrack, which was released by Total Sound. In 1973, Addar began to release the model kits. They commenced by releasing Cornelius, Dr. Zaius, General Aldo, and General Ursus in 1973. Addar was in the process of producing a Galen model kit when the company closed in late 1976. Also during 1973, Pressman released the ring toss game, spin n' color, and quick draw cartoon. In 1974, the remainder of the ape merchandise was released. Although there hasn't been any new licensed *Planet of the Apes* products released in over 20 years, there has been a large number of unlicensed items, particularly garage kits (unlicensed model kits) and T-shirts, released over the past few years. This is due to the increased popularity in collectibles from science-fiction films, particularly *Planet of the Apes*. You can also find the videos to all of the films, as well as the soundtrack to *Planet* on compact disc in your local video and music stores.

This guide primarily features both licensed and unlicensed American manufactured merchandise. Commingled in this guide are several foreign pieces, but these are certainly not representative of the complete available inventory from overseas. While some of the *Planet of the Apes* merchandise was produced in foreign countries (particularly the posters, action figures, and accessories), my primary purpose in creating this guide was to focus on the production of American merchandise. I hope you enjoy this in-depth look at the world of *Planet of the Apes* collectibles and memorabilia.

Please note that all the listed prices in this guide reflect a price range for items that are in mint condition — either mint on card (MOC), mint in package (MIP) or mint in box (MIB). Prices will vary greatly depending on the condition of the card, box, header card, or loose item. If the item is loose, the price will be considerably lower, depending on its condition. The prices listed are subject to change due to the popularity and scarcity of the items as well as increased interest in *Planet of the Apes*. It should also be noted that prices will fluctuate contingent upon your location. An item that brings $200 in New York, could actually be worth more or less in California. Be very careful when pursuing your ape collectibles, you don't want to be overcharged!

For some of the photographs, particularly the action figures and model kits, you will notice two price ranges listed under the caption. The first price is for an item in mint condition on a mint card or in a mint box. The second price is for items that are either loose or built. This will give you a better idea of the price range for these items. If a single price is listed, the referenced item is in mint condition. Please take note, all of the pictures in the collectibles section are from the author's personal collection, unless otherwise stated.

Action Figures

Description	Manufacture	Date	Price Range
8" Astronaut (1st series)	Mego	1974	$100-150
8" Cornelius (1st series)	Mego	1974	$75-125
8" Zira (1st series)	Mego	1974	$75-125
8" Dr. Zaius (1st series)	Mego	1974	$75-125
8" Soldier Ape (1st series)	Mego	1974	$75-125
8" Galen (2nd series)	Mego	1974	$75-125
8" Peter Burke (2nd series)	Mego	1974	$75-125
8" Alan Virdon (2nd series)	Mego	1974	$75-125
8" General Ursus (US release) (no helmet, black face on green card-2nd series)	Mego	1974	$75-125
8" General Urko (US release) (w/helmet on yellow card-2nd series)	Mego	1974	$75-125
8" General Ursus (Foreign release) (w/helmet on green card-2nd series)	Mego	1974	$75-125
8" General Urko (Foreign release) (no helmet, black face on yellow card-2nd series)	Mego	1974	$75-125

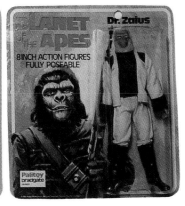

Three different card backs were made for the Mego action figures. The first series involved characters from the original *Planet of the Apes* film. The second series showed characters from the television series. The third card is from Britain, where the Mego figures were released under the brand name Palitoy, 1973-1974.

The back of the three different cards available for the Mego action figures. Pictured are series one, series two, and the Palitoy line, 1973-1974. The back of the Mego cards show the figures with the tree house playset in costumes that were never released.

1st Series 8" Cornelius figure by Mego, 1973. Mint on card (MOC): $75-$125. Loose: $30-50.

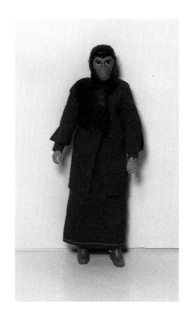

Loose 8" Zira figure by Mego, 1973. Mint on card (MOC): $75-125. Loose: $30-50.

2nd Series 8" General Urko on General Ursus green card by Mego, 1974. This was the foreign released figure. The General Urko US figure was released on a yellow card.   Mint on card (MOC): $75-150. Loose: $30-50.

8" Dr. Zaius figure by Palitoy, 1974. The carded Palitoy figures have a slightly higher value than the American Mego figures. Mint on card (MOC): $100-150. Loose: $30-50.

Loose 8" Soldier Ape and General Urko figures by Mego, 1974. The Soldier Ape figure comes with gloves and a rifle. The Urko figure also comes with a knife and rifle. Mint on card (MOC): $75-125 each. Loose: $30-50 each.

Loose 8" Astronaut figure by Mego, 1973. Figure also comes with a silver helmet with a blue visor. Mint on card (MOC): $100-150. Loose: $50-75.

Note: All of the above figures were also released in window, mailing boxes, but they are rarer and slightly higher in value. The figures were released in Britain under the Palitoy brand name. Although the figures are the same as Mego's, the cards are very different. Therefore, they are slightly higher in value. There were also figures released in Japan and Mexico. These figures are currently demanding $200-250 each.

The Cornelius and Galen figures look very similar. The best way to differentiate between the two figures is to look at their wrists. The Cornelius figure is held together by bendable plastic with a connecting metal joint on his wrist, whereas the Galen figure's wrist is made entirely of plastic. The Mego Corporation made this improvement between the release of the movie and television figures.

The soldier ape has three glove variations (full, half, and no glove). It should also be noted that Montgomery Wards sold the Astronaut figure as "Taylor" in its 1974 Christmas mail order catalog. All listed prices denote Mint on Card (MOC). The value for complete, loose figures ranges from $30-75 (depending on the figure and its accessories).

Dr. Zaius and Galen banks by Play Pal, 1974. $30-50 each.

Banks

Small Dr. Zaius Bank	Play Pal	1974	$30-50
Small Galen Bank	Play Pal	1974	$30-50
Large Cornelius Bank	A.J. Renzi	1974	$50-75
Large Dr. Zaius Bank	A.J. Renzi	1974	$50-75
Large General Ursus Bank	A.J. Renzi	1974	$50-75

Note: The large banks come in various colors.

Dr. Zaius, General Ursus, and Cornelius banks by A.J. Renzi, 1974. $50-75 each.

Belt Buckles/Ties

Alexander Belt Buckle	Lee Belt Co.	1974	$75-100
Cornelius Belt Buckle	Lee Belt Co.	1974	$75-100
Dr. Zaius Belt Buckle	Lee Belt Co.	1974	$75-100
General Ursus Belt Buckle	Lee Belt Co.	1974	$75-100
Alexander Western Bolo Tie	Lee Belt Co.	1974	$50-75
Cornelius Western Bolo Tie	Lee Belt Co.	1974	$50-75
Dr. Zaius Western Bolo Tie	Lee Belt Co.	1974	$50-75
General Ursus Western Bolo Tie	Lee Belt Co.	1974	$50-75

Note: Belts were also included with the belt buckles.

Dr. Zaius belt buckle by Lee Belt Company, 1974. $75-100.

Bendies

Bend N' Flex Astronaut	Mego	1974	$50-80
Bend N' Flex Cornelius	Mego	1974	$40-50
Bend N' Flex Galen	Mego	1974	$40-50
Bend N' Flex Soldier Ape	Mego	1974	$40-50
Bend N' Flex Dr. Zaius	Mego	1974	$40-50
Bend N' Flex Zira	Mego	1974	$40-80
Bend N' Flex Display Box	Mego	1974	$80-150

Soldier Ape bend n' flex by Mego, 1974. Mint on card (MOC): $40-50. Loose: $20-30.

Galen bend n' flex by Mego, 1974. Mint on card (MOC): $40-50. Loose: $20-30.

Loose Dr. Zaius bend n' flex by Mego, 1974. Mint on card (MOC): $40-50. Loose: $20-30.

Bike Accessories

Galen Safety Bike Flag	Cycle Safety	1974	$50-75
General Aldo Safety Bike Flag	Cycle Safety	1974	$50-75
Dr. Zaius Safety Bike Flag	Cycle Safety	1974	$50-75
Zira Safety Bike Flag	Cycle Safety	1974	$50-75

Book and Record Sets

Planet of the Apes	Power Records	1974	$20-40
Beneath the Planet of the Apes	Power Records	1974	$20-40
Escape from the Planet of the Apes	Power Records	1974	$20-40
Battle for the Planet of the Apes	Power Records	1974	$20-40

Note: A book and record set was not made for *Conquest of the Planet of the Apes*.

Planet of the Apes and *Beneath the Planet of the Apes* book and record sets by Power Records, 1974. $20-40.

Escape from the Planet of the Apes and *Battle for the Planet of the Apes* book and record sets by Power Records, 1974. $20-40.

CD-Rom

Planet of the Apes	Fox Interactive	1997	TBA

Note: This item had not been released at the time of this writing, so the price is undetermined. Keep your eyes open!

Collector Masks/Halloween Costumes

Gorilla Warrior w/Brown Face (1st Series)	Don Post	1974	$500-700
Cornelius w/Hair (1st Series)	Don Post	1974	$400-600
Dr. Zaius w/Hair (1st Series)	Don Post	1974	$400-600
Gorilla Warrior w/Hair (1st Series)	Don Post	1974	$400-600
Zira w/Hair (1st Series)	Don Post	1974	$600-700
Cornelius w/Hair (2nd Series)	Don Post	1983	$250-350
Dr. Zaius w/Hair (2nd Series)	Don Post	1983	$250-350
General Aldo w/Hair (2nd Series)	Don Post	1983	$250-350
Gorilla Warrior w/Hair (2nd Series)	Don Post	1983	$250-350
Cornelius w/Sculpted Hair	Don Post	1974	$200-300
Dr. Zaius w/Sculpted Hair	Don Post	1974	$200-300
Gorilla Warrior w/Sculpted Hair	Don Post	1974	$200-300
Caesar Mask (closed eyes)	Matthew Sotis	1995	$200-250
Gorilla Mask (closed eyes)	Matthew Sotis	1996	$250-300
Mutant Mask (closed eyes)	Matthew Sotis	1995	$200-250
Dr. Zaius Mask (open eyes)	Matthew Sotis	1997	$300-350
Dr. Zira Mask (open eyes)	Matthew Sotis	1996	$300-350
Dr. Zaius Halloween Costume	Ben Copper	1974	$40-75
Galen Halloween Costume	Ben Copper	1974	$40-75
Lisa Halloween Costume	Ben Copper	1974	$40-75
Warrior Halloween Costume	Ben Copper	1974	$40-75
Caesar Halloween Costume	Ben Cooper	1974	$40-75
Galen Halloween Mask ($1.19)	Ben Copper	1974	$25-50
Dr. Zaius Halloween Mask ($1.19)	Ben Cooper	1974	$25-50
Warrior Halloween Mask ($1.19)	Ben Cooper	1974	$25-50
Lisa Halloween Mask ($.69)	Ben Cooper	1974	$25-50
Playset Mask w/Hair	Ben Cooper	1974	$50-75
Gorilla Mask w/Hair	Illusive Concepts	1995	$40-60
Gorilla Mask w/Sculpted Hair	Illusive Concepts	1995	$25-40
Gorilla Guard Costume	Illusive Concepts	1995	$40-60
Black-Haired Ape w/Neon Lips	Unknown	1970s	$5-10

Note: The masks made by Matthew Sotis are cast from the original molds that were used in the film.

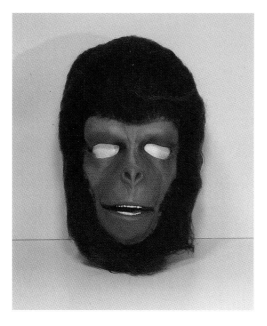

1st series Cornelius mask by Don Post, 1974. $400-600.

2nd series Dr. Zaius mask by Don Post, 1983. $250-350.

2nd series General Aldo mask by Don Post, 1983. $250-350.

Mutant human and Caesar masks by Matthew Sotis, 1995. *Courtesy of Matthew Sotis*. These masks are made from the mold that was used in the film. $200-250 each.

Dr. Zaius mask by Matthew Sotis, 1997. *Courtesy of Matthew Sotis*. This mask was made from a mold used in the film. $300-350.

Gorilla mask by Illusive Concepts, 1995. $40-60.

Dr. Zaius Halloween costume by Ben Cooper, 1974. $40-75.

Gorilla guard costume by Illusive Concepts, 1995. $40-60.

Dr. Zaius Halloween costume by Ben Cooper, 1974. Loose: $20-30.

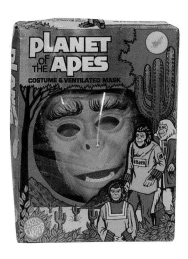

Galen Halloween costume by Ben Cooper, 1974. $40-75.

Galen Halloween costume by Ben Cooper, 1974. Loose: $20-30.

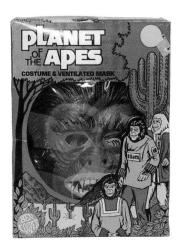

Warrior Halloween costume by Ben Cooper, 1974. $40-75.

Dr. Zaius Halloween mask by Ben Cooper, 1974. $25-50.

Coloring/Activity Books

Coloring/Activity Books (set of 6)	Artcraft	1974	$10-15 ea. $60-90

Coloring/Activity Book
  Display Unit
  (includes 90 coloring books)
	Artcraft	1974	$500-1000

Giant Picture Activity Book	Artcraft	1974	$10-15

Warrior Halloween costume by Ben Cooper, 1974. Loose: $20-30.

Coloring/activity books by Artcraft, 1974. $10-15 each.

Coloring/activity books by Artcraft, 1974. $10-15 each.

Playset mask with hair by Ben Cooper, 1974. $50-75.

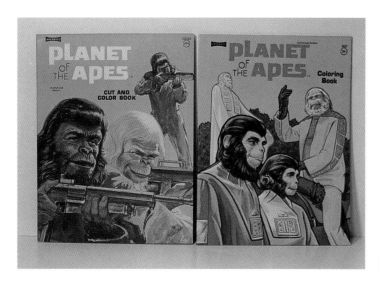

Coloring/activity books by Artcraft, 1974. $10-15 each.

The Forbidden Zone	Adventure	1991	$5-10 ea.
(set of 4)			$30-40
Ape Nation	Adventure	1991	$5-10 ea.
(set of 4)			$30-40
A Day on the Planet of the Apes	Adventure	1992	$5-10
Sins of the Father #1	Adventure	1992	$5-10
POTA "Monkey Planet"	Charles		
	Marshall	1991	$15-20
Nova Comes Along Storyboard	Adventure	1990	$20-30
Beneath the Planet of the Apes	Gold Key	1974	
(with apes protest poster)			$25-50
(without apes protest poster)			$10-25

Giant picture activity book by Artcraft, 1974. $10-15.

Comic magazines #1 & 2 by Marvel, 1974. $10-15 each.

Comics

Planet of the Apes			
Comic Magazine	Marvel	1974	$10-15 ea.
(set of 29)			$275-400
Adventure on the Planet			
of the Apes	Marvel	1975	$10-15 ea.
(set of 11)			$100-150
Planet of the Apes Limited			
Collectors Edition	Adventure	1990	$20-40
Planet of the Apes	Adventure	1990	$5-10 ea.
(set of 24)			$150-200
Urchaks Folly	Adventure	1990	$5-10 ea.
(set of 4)			$30-40
Terror on the Planet of the Apes	Adventure	1990	$5-10 ea.
(set of 4)			$30-40
Blood of the Apes	Adventure	1990	$5-10 ea.
(set of 4)			$30-40
Ape City	Adventure	1991	$5-10 ea.
(set of 4)			$30-40

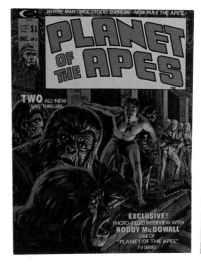

Comic magazines #3 & 4 by Marvel, 1974. $10-15 each.

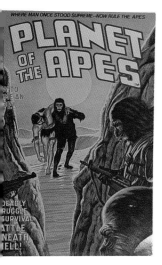

Comic magazines #5 & 6 by Marvel, 1974. $10-15 each.

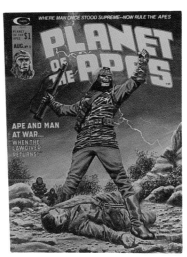

Comic magazines #11 & 12 by Marvel, 1974. $10-15 each.

Comic magazines #7 & 8 by Marvel, 1974. $10-15 each.

Comic magazines #9 & 10 by Marvel, 1974. $10-15 each.

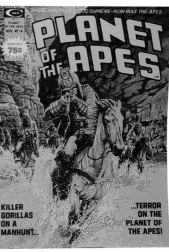

Comic magazines #13 & 14 by Marvel, 1974. $10-15 each.

Comic magazines #15 & 16 by Marvel, 1974. $10-15 each.

Comic magazines # 22 & 23 by Marvel, 1974. $10-15 each.

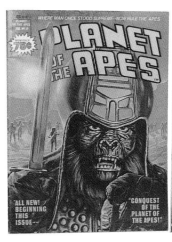

Comic magazines #17 & 18 by Marvel, 1974. $10-15 each.

Comic magazines #24 & 25 by Marvel, 1974. $10-15 each.

Comic magazines #19 & 21 by Marvel, 1974. $10-15 each.

Comic magazines #26 & 27 by Marvel, 1974. $10-15 each.

Comic magazines #28 & 29 by Marvel, 1974. $10-15 each.

Adventures on the Planet of the Apes comics #7 & 11 by Marvel, 1975. $10-15 each.

Adventures on the Planet of the Apes comics #1 & 2 by Marvel, 1975. $10-15 each.

Adventures on the Planet of the Apes comics #4 & 6 by Marvel, 1975. $10-15 each.

Planet of the Apes comics #1 & 2 by Adventure Comics, 1990. $5-10 each.

Planet of the Apes comics #3 & 4 by Adventure Comics, 1990. $5-10 each.

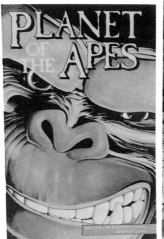

Planet of the Apes comics #1 & 5 by Adventure Comics, 1990. $5-10 each.

Beneath the Planet of the Apes comic by Gold Key, 1974. $25-50. The price range without the ape protest poster is $10-25.

Planet of the Apes comics #6 & 7 by Adventure Comics, 1990. $5-10 each.

Food/Stickers/Jewelry

Candy Boxes	Phoenix	1974	$20-30 ea.
(set of 8)			$250-350
Candy Box #1 (a)	Phoenix	1974	$75-100
Candy Box #2 (b)	Phoenix	1974	$75-100
Candy Boxes Display Box	Phoenix	1974	$250-300
Cornelius Lollipop (Chocolate)	Unknown	1974	$150-200
Dr. Zaius Lollipop (Chocolate)	Unknown	1974	$150-200
General Ursus Lollipop			
(Chocolate)	Unknown	1974	$150-200
Small 1 1/2" - 1 3/4"			
Tall Stickers	Mego	1974	$15-20 ea.
(set of 5 8" Mego figures)			$50-100
Large 6 1/2" - 7" Tall Stickers	Mego	1974	$15-20 ea.
(set of 5 8" Mego figures)			$50-100
Rings (British)	Stan Lee	1974	$300-400 ea.
(set of 5)			$1,500-2,000
Ring Display Box			
(British)	Stan Lee	1974	$1,250-1,500
Dr. Zaius Key Chain			
(rubber figure)	Unknown	1974	$25-75
Vending Machine Necklaces	Mego	1974	$20-30 ea.
(set of 5 Mego figure heads)			$100-150
Vending Machine Store Display	Mego	1974	$2,000-2,500

(display for the Mego stickers and medallions)

a - picture variation: front = Caesar chained; back = frame says "gorilla"
b - color variation: color is dark orange and purple

Planet of the Apes comics #12 & 15 by Adventure Comics, 1990. $5-10 each.

Front of candy boxes #2, 3, and 5 by Phoenix, 1974. $20-30 each.

Back of candy boxes #6, 7, and 8 by Phoenix, 1974. $20-30 each.

Back of candy boxes #2, 3, and 5 by Phoenix, 1974. $20-30 each.

Tall Cornelius sticker by Mego, 1974. $15-20.

Front of candy boxes #6, 7, and 8 by Phoenix, 1974. $20-30 each.

Vending machine necklace set of Zira, Dr. Zaius, Astronaut, Soldier Ape, and Cornelius by Mego, 1974. $20-30 each. Set of 5: $100-150.

Garbage Cans

| Tall, Round w/Statue of Liberty | Cheinco | 1974 | $75-125 |
| Small, Oval w/Humans in Cage | Cheinco | 1974 | $75-125 |

Guns and other Weapons

Archery Set	H.G. Toys	1974	$100-150
Automatic Pellet Rifle	Larami	1974	$75-125
Fanner Gun	Mattel	1974	$100-150
Pellet Shooting Walkie Talkie	Larami	1974	$50-75
Pop N' Spin Pistol & Target Set	Larami	1974	$100-125
Rapid Fire Rifle w/ape mask	Mattel	1974	$250-350
Tommy Burst Sub-Machine			
Gun w/ape mask	Mattel	1974	$250-300
Dr. Zaius Water Gun	AHI	1974	$100-150
Galen Water Gun	AHI	1974	$100-150

Note: The Automatic Pellet Rifle was available in blue, brown, and white.

Garbage can by Cheinco, 1974. $75-125.

Front of garbage can by Cheinco, 1974. $75-125.

Automatic pellet rifle by Larami, 1974. The rifle was available in blue, brown, and white. $75-125.

Back of garbage can by Cheinco, 1974.

Tommy burst sub-machine gun by Mattel, 1974. The gun also came with an ape mask. Mint in box (MIB): $250-300. Loose: $100-125.

Hardcover Books

Planet of the Apes w/sleeve	Pierre Boulle	1964	$20-30
Planet of the Apes:			
As American Myth	Eric Greene	1995	$20-25
1975 British Annual	Brown Watson	1975	$20-30
1976 British Annual	Brown Watson	1976	$20-30
1977 British Annual	Brown Watson	1977	$20-30
TV Series #1 (Man the			
Fugitive)	George Effinger	1974	$10-20
The Actor's Life:			
Journals 1956-1976	Charlton Heston	1970s	$20-30
In the Arena: An Autobiography	Charlton Heston	1996	$20-30
Making of a Monster	Al Taylor	1980	$20-25
Loose in the Kitchen	Kim Hunter	1975	$20-25
(an autobiographical cookbook)			
Pictorial History of Sci-Fi Films	David Shipman	1978	$10-20
Science Fiction Films	Robert Cross	1985	$10-20

Galen water gun by AHI, 1974. Mint in package (MIP): $100-150. Loose: $50-100.

Planet of the Apes hard cover novel by Pierre Boulle, 1964. $20-30.

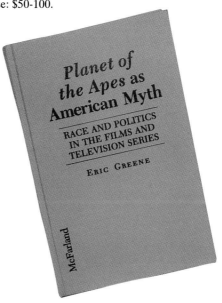

Planet of the Apes: As American Myth book by Eric Greene, 1995. $20-25.

British annual by Brown Watson, 1975. $20-30.

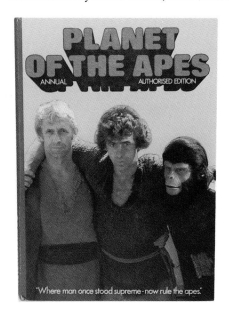

British annual by Brown Watson, 1976. $20-30.

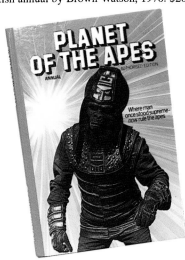

British annual by Brown Watson, 1977. $20-30.

Kitchen Related Products

Bowl	Deka	1974	$10-20
Cup (10 oz.)	Deka	1974	$10-20
Plate	Deka	1974	$20-30
Tumbler	Deka	1974	$15-30

Note: The complete set of four pieces sells for $60-100.

Bowl and cup by Deka, 1974. $10-20 each.

Kites

Graphic of Ape Head ($1.00)	Hi-Flyer	1974	$50-75
Graphic of Full Ape ($1.49)	Hi-Flyer	1974	$50-75

Kite with graphic of full ape by Hi-Flyer. 1974. $50-75.

Laser Discs

Planet of the Apes	CBS/Fox	1990s	$75-100
Beneath the Planet of the Apes	CBS/Fox	1990s	$50-75
Escape from the Planet of the Apes	CBS/Fox	1990s	$50-75
Conquest from the Planet of the Apes	CBS/Fox	1990s	$50-75
Planet of the Apes (Video-Disc)	RCA	1980s	$75-100

Note: Battle for the Planet of the Apes was not released on laser disc in the United States. The complete set of ape movies were available on laser disc in letterbox format in Japan. I have seen this set advertised in *Toy Shop* and at toy shows for $300-$400.

Magazines and Other Paper Products

American Cinematographer (April 1968)	Amer. Cine.	1968	$10-15
Ape: Monster of the Movies (also titled Ape: The Kingdom of Kong)	David Annan	1975	$20-30
The Art of the Cinematographer	Leonard Maltin	1971	$10-20
Big Screen Scene Showguide	Big Screen	1968	$15-20
Castle of Frankenstein #13	Castle of Frank.	1969	$10-15
Castle of Frankenstein #23	Castle of Frank.	1973	$5-10
Cinefantastique (Summer 1972)	Cinefantastique	1972	$20-30
Cinescape (November 1996)	Cinescape	1996	$5-10
Cinescape (January/February)	Cinescape	1997	$5-10
Cracked #123	Cracked	1974	$5-10
Details (March 1996)	Details	1996	$5-10
Entertainment Weekly (2/9/96)	Ent. Weekly	1996	$4-8
Entertainment Weekly (5/3/96)	Ent. Weekly	1996	$4-8
Epilog #1	Epilog	1990	$5-10
Epilog (January 1992)	Epilog	1992	$5-10
Epilog (March 1993)	Epilog	1993	$5-10
Epilog (July/Aug 1993)	Epilog	1993	$5-10
Famous Monsters of Filmland #52	Famous Monsters	1970	$10-15
Famous Monsters of Filmland #80	Famous Monsters	1971	$10-15
Famous Monsters of Filmland #85	Famous Monsters	1971	$10-15
Famous Monsters of Filmland #108	Famous Monsters		$5-10
Fangoria #6	Fangoria	1974	$10-15
Film Comment (November 1995)	Film Comment	1995	$5-10
Film Review (May 1997)	Film Review	1997	$5-10
Films in Review (Escape Cover)	Unknown	1970s	$20-30
Gastly Giggles Booklet (behind the scenes pictures w/word balloon gags)	Unknown	1975	$125-150
A Guide for Teachers & Students	William Leader	1970s	$5-15
Mad Magazine #157	Mad Magazine	1973	$5-10
Media & Methods (Review of Planet)	M&M	1973	$20-30
The Monster Times #11	Monster Times	1972	$10-15
The Monster Times #12	Monster Times	1972	$10-15
The Monster Times #17	Monster Times	1970s	$5-10
The Monster Times #18	Monster Times	1970s	$5-10
The Monster Times #33	Monster Times	1974	$10-15
The Monster Times #36	Monster Times	1970s	$5-10
The Monster Times #37	Monster Times	1974	$10-15
The Monster Times #38	Monster Times	1970s	$5-10
The Monster Times #39	Monster Times	1975	$10-15

Planet of the Apes and *Beneath the Planet of the Apes* laser discs by CBS/Fox, 1990s. *Courtesy of Matthew Sotis.* $75-100 and $50-75, respectively.

Escape from the Planet of the Apes and *Conquest of the Planet of the Apes* laser discs by CBS/Fox, 1990s. *Courtesy of Matthew Sotis.* $50-75 each.

Big Screen Scene Showguide, 1968. $15-20.

The Monster Times #41	*Monster Times*	1970s	$5-10
Movie Monsters #2	*Movie Monsters*	1975	$5-10
Scary Monsters Yearbook 1997 #5	*Scary Monsters*	1997	$8-10
Scary Monsters #22	*Scary Monsters*	1997	$5-10
Scary Monsters #23	*Scary Monsters*	1997	$5-10
Scary Monsters #24	*Scary Monsters*	1997	$5-10
Scary Monsters #25	*Scary Monsters*	1997	$5-10
Scholastic Scope (September 1973)	*Scholastic*	1973	$20-30
Sci-Fi Entertainment (June 1996)	*Sci-Fi Ent.*	1996	$5-10
Sci-Fi Entertainment (April 1997)	*Sci-Fi Ent.*	1997	$5-10
Sci-Fi Now	Alan Frank	1978	$10-15
Sci-Fi Universe #1	*Sci-Fi Universe*	1994	$10-15
Starlog #105	Starlog Press	1985	$5-10
Starlog #117	Starlog Press	1987	$5-10
Starlog #160	Starlog Press	1990s	$5-10
Starlog #213	Starlog Press	1995	$5-10
World of Horror #5	British	1975	$10-15
Planet of the Apes Official Adaptation	Malibu Graphics	1990	$15-20
Beneath the POTA Official Adaptation	Malibu Graphics	1991	$10-15
Escape from the POTA Adaptation	Malibu Graphics	1991	$10-15
Posterbook Magazine (British) (folds into General Urko poster)	Top Sellers	1974	$20-30
Roddy McDowall-An Unauthorized Biography (25 page booklet about Roddy McDowall with several photos in ape makeup)	Unknown	1970s	$20-30
Great Science Fiction from the Movies (photo from *Planet of the Apes* on the cover)	Edward Edelson	1976	$10-15

Note: This is just a sample of some of the magazines and books that contained covers or articles on *Planet of the Apes*. There are many more magazines that contained articles or reviews on the films. However, my intention was to include those magazines, that I was aware of, with *Planet of the Apes* on the cover or which contained an interesting article on *Planet of the Apes*.

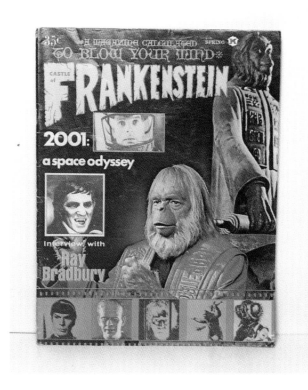

Dr. Zaius on the cover of *Castle of Frankenstein* #13, 1969. $10-15.

Return to the Planet of the Apes on the cover of *Castle of Frankenstein* #23, 1973. $5-10.

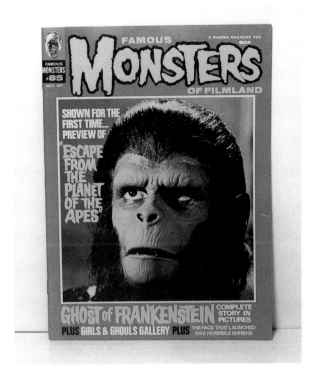

Special Issue on Planet of the Apes in *Cinefantastique* #2, 1972. In my opinion, this is one of the finest pieces written on the *Planet of the Apes*. It is packed with interviews from everyone who contributed to the film. $20-30.

Cornelius from *Escape from the Planet of the Apes* on the cover of *Famous Monsters of Filmland* #85, 1971. $10-15.

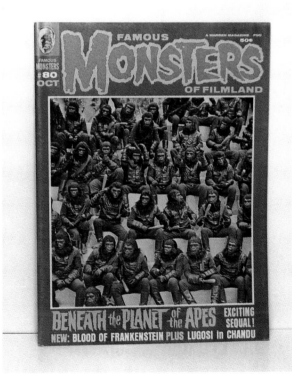

Stadium scene from *Beneath the Planet of the Apes* on the cover of *Famous Monsters of Filmland* #80, 1970. $10-15.

Taylor being restrained by gorilla soldiers on the cover of *The Monster Times* #11, 1972. $10-15.

Special issues on *Planet of the Apes* in *Cracked* #123 and *Mad* #157, 1974. $5-10 each.

A Study Guide for Teachers and Students on the Planet of the Apes by William Leader, 1970s. $5-15.

Marcus on the cover of *The Monster Times* #33, 1972. $10-15.

Battle for the Planet of the Apes cover on *Scholastic Scope* #2, 1973. $20-30.

Dr. Zaius on the cover of *Movie Monsters* #2, 1975. $5-10.

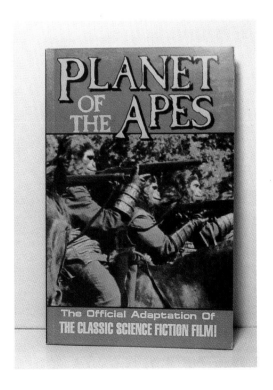

Battle for the Planet of the Apes cover on *World of Horror* #5, 1975. $10-15.

Planet of the Apes Official Adaptation by Malibu Graphics, 1990. $15-20.

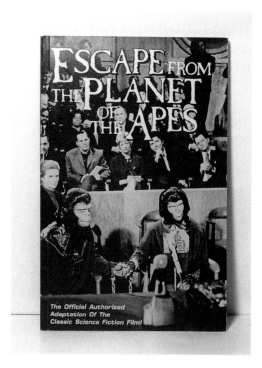

Escape from the Planet of the Apes Official Adaptation by Malibu Graphics, 1990. $10-15.

Caesar Rubber Dangle Figure	Ben Cooper	1973	$10-15
Warrior Rubber Dangle Figure	Ben Cooper	1973	$10-15
Rubber Dangle Display Box	Ben Cooper	1973	$75-100
12" Autograph Dr. Zaius Doll	Commonwealth	1974	$75-100
12" Autograph Galen Doll	Commonwealth	1974	$75-100
Dr. Zaius Bean Bag Doll	Commonwealth	1974	$40-80
Galen Bean Bag Doll	Commonwealth	1974	$40-80
9" Dr. Zaius (w/tag)	Well-Made Toys	1974	$75-100
12" Dr. Zaius (w/box)	Well-Made Toys	1974	$100-150
9" Galen (w/tag)	Well-Made Toys	1974	$75-100
12" Galen (w/box)	Well-Made Toys	1974	$100-150
Dr. Zaius Dangle Head	Well-Made Toys	1974	$50-75
Galen Dangle Head	Well-Made Toys	1974	$50-75
Sky Diving Parachutist, Dr. Zaius	AHI	1974	$25-50
Sky Diving Parachutist, Galen	AHI	1974	$25-50
Wind-Up Galen (on horse)	AHI	1974	$100-150
Wind-Up Dr. Zaius (on horse)	AHI	1974	$100-150
Little Walker/Wind-Up Galen	AHI	1974	$100-150
Little Walker/Wind-Up Dr. Zaius	AHI	1974	$100-150
Stunt Cycle, Galen	AHI	1974	$100-150
Stunt Cycle, Dr. Zaius	AHI	1974	$100-150
Zoom Cycle, Galen	AHI	1974	$100-150
Zoom Cycle, Dr. Zaius	AHI	1974	$100-150

Caesar and warrior rubber dangle figures by Ben Cooper, 1973. $10-15 each.

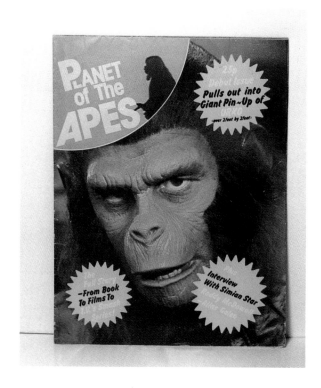

Posterbook magazine by Top Sellers, 1974. The magazine folds out into a poster of General Urko. $20-30.

12" Dr. Zaius autograph doll by Commonwealth, 1974. Mint in package (MIP): $75-100. Loose: $25-50.

Dr. Zaius Remote Control on Horse	AHI	1974	$150-200
Galen Remote Control on Horse	AHI	1974	$150-200
17" Galen Stuffed Doll	Carnival Toys	1974	$200-250
17" Dr. Zaius Stuffed Doll	Carnival Toys	1974	$200-250
8" Action Apeman Orangutan	AHI	1974	$75-100
8" Action Apeman in Camouflage	AHI	1974	$75-100
8" Artemus Astro Ape	Seaside	1974	$75-100
8" Dr. Zorma Astro Ape	Seaside	1974	$75-100
8" Myra Astro Ape	Seaside	1974	$75-100
8" Warrior Ape	Seaside	1974	$75-100
9" Simple Simian Doll	Knickerbocker	1970s	$35-50
62" Jointed Galen	Our Way	1974	$75-100
8" Black Mutant Custom Figure	Matthew Sotis	1996	$100-125
8" Brent Custom Figure	Matthew Sotis	1995	$50-75
8" Conquest Chimpanzee Custom Figure	Matthew Sotis	1996	$80-100
8" Conquest Gorilla Custom Figure	Matthew Sotis	1996	$80-100
8" Conquest Orangutan Custom Figure	Matthew Sotis	1996	$80-100
8" Dummied Dodge Custom Figure	Matthew Sotis	1995	$50-75
8" Fatman Mutant Custom Figure	Matthew Sotis	1996	$100-125
8" Female Gorilla Custom Figure	Matthew Sotis	1997	$80-100
8" General Urko Custom Figure	Matthew Sotis	1996	$100-125
8" Gorilla Sergeant Custom Figure	Matthew Sotis	1995	$50-75
8" Julius Custom Figure	Matthew Sotis	1996	$80-100
8" Lobotomized Landon Custom Figure	Matthew Sotis	1995	$50-75
8" Dr. Honorius Custome Figure	Matthew Sotis	1997	$80-100
8" Mutant Mendez Custom Figure	Matthew Sotis	1995	$50-75
8" Steambath General Ursus	Matthew Sotis	1996	$80-100
8" Taylor Custom Figure	Matthew Sotis	1996	$80-100
8" Dr. Zaius Custom Figure	Matthew Sotis	1997	$80-100
Apejoe General Ursus	P. Moreno	1996	$175-200

Dr. Zaius and Galen sky diving parachutists by AHI, 1974. $25-50 each.

Galen wind-up figure on horse by AHI, 1974. Mint on card (MOC): $100-150. Loose: $50-75.

12" Galen plush doll by Well-Made Toys, 1974. Mint in box (MIB): $100-150. Loose: $75-100.

Dr. Zaius little walker wind-up figure by AHI, 1974. Mint on card (MOC): $100-150. Loose: $50-75.

Giant jointed Galen by Our Way, 1974. Mint in package (MIP): $75-100. Loose: $50-75.

Galen little walker wind-up figure by AHI, 1974. Figure also comes with a wind-up key. Mint on card (MOC): $100-150. Loose: $50-75.

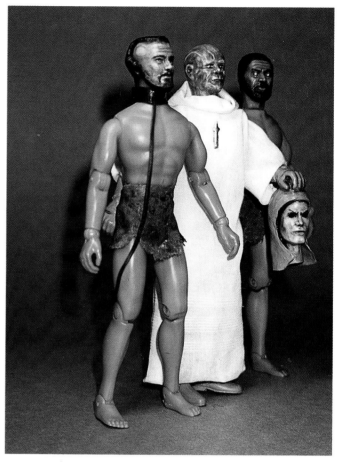

8" custom Landon, mutant human, and Dodge figures by Matthew Sotis, 1995. *Courtesy of Matthew Sotis.* $50-75 each.

8" custom gorilla Sergeant figure by Matthew Sotis, 1995. *Courtesy of Matthew Sotis.* $50-75.

8" custom Taylor figure by Matthew Sotis, 1996. *Courtesy of Matthew Sotis.* $80-100.

8" custom female gorilla figure by Matthew Sotis, 1997. There was a female gorilla costumes made, but it was never used in any of the films. *Courtesy of Matthew Sotis.* $80-100.

8" custom steambath General Ursus figure by Matthew Sotis, 1996. *Courtesy of Matthew Sotis.* $80-100.

8" custom Julius figure with long sleeves by Matthew Sotis, 1996. *Courtesy of Matthew Sotis.* $80-100.

8" custom Dr. Zaius figure by Matthew Sotis, 1997. *Courtesy of Matthew Sotis.* $80-100.

Fun-doh & modeling molds by Chemtoy, 1974. $100-125.

Apejoe Cornelius	P. Moreno	1996	$175-200
Apejoe Zira	P. Moreno	1996	$175-200
Apejoe Dr. Zaius (TV series)	P. Moreno	1996	$175-200
Apejoe Dr. Zaius (Movie)	P. Moreno	1996	$175-200
Apejoe Julius	P. Moreno	1996	$175-200
Apejoe General Aldo	P. Moreno	1996	$175-200
Apejoe Taylor	P. Moreno	1996	$175-200
Apejoe Mutant Human	P. Moreno	1996	$175-200

Note: A majority of the custom Mego figures are also available with a custom made box. The price for a boxed figure ranges from $150-225 for each figure. To the best of my knowledge, the custom Mego's are available from two sources. Matthew Sotis makes all of the figures loose and at very reasonable prices. Chris Sutton sells the figures with the custom made boxes. The prices for these figures are slightly higher. Several of the custom figures come with custom accessories (guns, dog tags, club) and outfits. If any one is interested in finding out more information about the custom figures or masks, you can contact Matthew Sotis at P.O. Box 1079, Medford, New York 11763.

The costumes for the custom figures from *Conquest* include a green jumpsuit for the chimpanzee, red jumpsuit for the gorilla, and a yellow jumpsuit for the orangutan. The Julius custom figure is available in two styles. One comes with a short sleeve costume exposing his hairy arms, and the other comes with a long sleeve costume, covering his arms. You may be wondering why there is a female gorilla, since one does not appear in any of the films. There was, in fact, a costume made for the female gorilla character, but it was never used. Further, the Apejoe figures are the size of G.I. Joe's and most of them include custom accessories (scrolls, doll, club), as well as custom costumes.

Miscellaneous Merchandise

A.M. Radio w/photo from			
Escape	Intraptor, Inc.	1974	$200-400
Beach Ball (inflatable)	AHI	1974	$125-150
Beanbag Chair	Unknown	1974	$200-250
Blueprints (set of 4)	20th Century-		
	Fox	1990s	$50-75
Bommerangutang	Larami	1974	$75-100
Billions of Bubbles	Larami	1974	$75-125
Dr. Zaius Figural Bubble Blower	Hot Items, Inc.	1974	$100-200
Press N' Blow Bubbles	Hot Items, Inc.	1974	$75-125
Chimp-Scope	Larami	1974	$50-75
Club Bat & Ball (w/header card)	H.G. Toys	1974	$75-100
Copycast casting factory	Strawberry		
	Fayre	1975	$75-150
Comforter (blanket)	Unknown	1974	$200-250
Drum Set	Noble & Cooley	1974	$250-300
Eye Spies	Larami	1974	$75-100
Face Ball	Amsco	1974	$75-100
Fun-Doh Modeling Molds	Chemtoy	1974	$100-125
Giggle Gob Hat	Unknown	1975	$75-100
Gorilla Scope	Larami	1974	$50-75
Inflatable Galen (19")	Ideal	1974	$200-250
Inflatable Dr. Zaius (19")	Ideal	1974	$200-250
Inflatable General Urko (19")	Ideal	1974	$200-250
Inter-Planetary Ape Phone	Larami	1974	$30-50
Light Switch Plate (British)	Unknown	1974	$50-100
Lunchbox with thermos	Aladdin	1974	$150-175
Lunchbox without thermos	Aladdin	1974	$100-125
Thermos	Aladdin	1974	$40-50

Magic Slate	Saalfield	1974	$100-125
Monkey Missiles	Larami	1975	$25-45 ea.
(set of 3)			$75-135
Monkey Shines Flashlight	Larami	1974	$75-100
Movie Viewer	Chemtoy	1974	$75-100
Periscope (blue)	Winner		
	Promotions	1974	$100-125
Pillow	Commonwealth	1974	$75-125
Pillow (w/ hair on back)	Toy & Novelty	1974	$100-150
Plaster Cornelius Statue	Tuscany Studio	1973	$150-250
Plaster Zera Statue			
(Zira misspelled)	Tuscany Studio	1973	$150-250
Play Feet	Commonwealth	1974	$75-150
Dr. Zaius Hand Puppet	Commonwealth	1974	$50-75
Galen Hand Puppet	Commonwealth	1974	$50-75
Silly Soap	Hot Items, Inc.	1974	$25-50
Sleeping Bag	Unknown	1974	$200-250
Sonic Zooms	Larami	1974	$40-60
Space Scope	Larami	1974	$50-75
Surf Rider (inflatable)	AHI	1974	$125-150
Wading Pool (inflatable)	AHI	1974	$125-150
Wrapping Paper	Unknown	1975	$200-250
General Urko 3-D Wall Plaque	Whiting	1974	$100-125
Zing-Wing Frisbee			
(blue or green)	AHI	1974	$100-125
			ea.

Note: The blueprints were sold on QVC and include: ape alphabet, buildings, amphitheater, and spacecraft. When you purchased them, you also received a letter of authenticity and an apes T-shirt with a graphic of the movie poster from *Planet*.

Inflatable General Urko doll by Ideal, 1974. Mint in package (MIP): $200-250. Loose: $100-125.

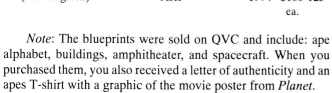

Chimp-scope by Larami, 1974. $50-75.

Inter-planetary ape phone by Larami, 1974. $30-50.

Giggle gob hat by an unknown manufacturer, 1975. $75-100.

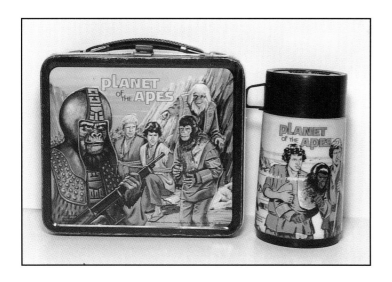

Front of lunch box with thermos by Aladdin, 1974. $150-175.

Set of three monkey missiles by Larami, 1975. $75-135 for set. $25-45 each.

Back of lunch box with thermos by Aladdin, 1974.

Front of periscope by Winner Promotions, 1974. $100-125.

Monkey shines flashlight by Larami, 1974. Mint on card (MOC): $75-100. Loose: $25-50.

Back of periscope by Winner Promotions, 1974.

Dr. Zaius hand puppet by Commonwealth, 1974. Mint in package (MIP): $50-75. Loose: $20-40.

General Urko 3-D wall plaque by Whiting, 1974. $100-125.

Sleeping bag by an unknown manufacturer, 1974. $200-250.

Zing-wing frisbee by AHI, 1974. The frisbee was available in blue or green. Mint in package (MIP): $100-125. Loose: $50-75.

Silly soap by Hot Items, Inc., 1974. $25-50.

Front & back of custom infantry field pack by Matthew Sotis, 1997. Pack includes backpack, rifle, flag, and rope. *Courtesy of Matthew Sotis.* $40-60.

Miscellaneous Unlicensed Merchandise

Baseball cap w/ANSA patch	P. Moreno	1996	$10-15
Planet of the Grapes sticker	Wacky Packages	1970s	$1-3
Planet of the Grapes magnet	Unknown	1996	$5-10
Cornelius Magnet	Unknown	1993	$10-15
Baby Milo Magnet	Unknown	1993	$10-15
Dr. Zaius Magnet	Unknown	1993	$10-15
Zira Magnet	Unknown	1993	$10-15
Infantry Field Pack	Matthew Sotis	1997	$40-60
Magnet	Rialto Movie	1996	$10-15
6" Vacu-Form ANSA Spacecraft	S.F.M.A.	1980s	$100-125
12" Scratch Built Resin Spacecraft	Unknown	1980s	$75-100
Dr. Zaius (small gold plastic figure)	Unknown	1974	$40-50
Dr. Zaius Plastic Squirting Ring (brown with pink water squirter)	Unknown	1974	$20-25
Gorilla Soldier (small plastic figure)	HTLV	1992	$10-15

Mix 'N Molds

Cornelius	Catalog Shoppe	1974	$40-60
Dr. Zaius (blue suit with boots)	Catalog Shoppe	1974	$40-60
Dr. Zaius (wearing sandals)	Catalog Shoppe	1974	$40-60
Galen	Catalog Shoppe	1974	$40-60
General Urko	Catalog Shoppe	1974	$40-60
Peter Burke	Catalog Shoppe	1974	$40-60
Alan Virdon	Catalog Shoppe	1974	$40-60

12" scratch built resin spacecraft by an unknown manufacturer, 1980s. $75-100.

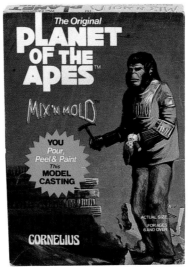
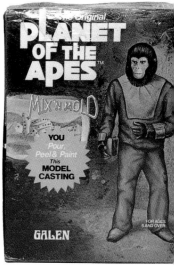

Cornelius and Galen mix 'n molds by Catalog Shoppe, 1974. $40-60 each.

Model Kits/Garage Kits

Cornelius	Addar	1973	$50-75
Dr. Zaius	Addar	1973	$50-75
Zira	Addar	1974	$50-75
General Ursus	Addar	1973	$50-75
General Aldo	Addar	1973	$50-75
Caesar	Addar	1974	$60-80
Stallion & Soldier	Addar	1974	$200-250
Treehouse	Addar	1975	$40-60
Jail Wagon	Addar	1975	$40-60
Cornfield Roundup	Addar	1975	$40-60
General Urko Bust (large)	Unknown	1995	$100-125
General Urko Bust (small)	Unknown	1996	$40-60
Cornelius with ruins	Resins from the Grave	1995	$100-125
General with slave girl	Unknown	1995	$100-150
Gorilla Soldier with dead human	Unknown	1996	$100-150
The Hunt (gorilla soldier)	Vic Door	1995	$60-80
The General (Ursus)	Vic Door	1995	$60-80
7" Cornelius Poly Resin Statue (holding skull/sitting on a stack of books)	Unknown	1996	$50-75
Soldier Ape (deformed resin kit)	Japan	1970s	$50-100
Dr. Zaius Bust (small)	Resinator	1995	$15-20
Cornelius Bust (small)	Resinator	1995	$15-20
Gorilla Bust (small)	Resinator	1995	$15-20
Cornelius	AOCP	1996	$50-75
Cornelius (Astronaut outfit)	AOCP	1996	$50-75
Dr. Zaius	AOCP	1996	$50-75
Zira	AOCP	1996	$50-75
Gorilla w/rifle	AOCP	1996	$50-75

Note: AOCP stands for Attack of the Clay People.

Dr. Zaius mix 'n molds by Catalog Shoppe, 1974. The two variations include one from the movie and one from the television series. $40-60 each.

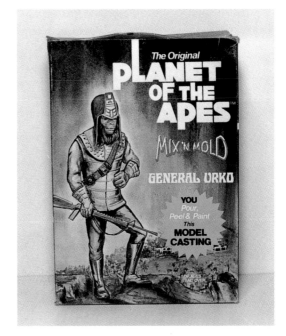

General Urko mix 'n mold by Catalog Shoppe, 1974. $40-60.

Planet of the Apes model kits by Addar, 1973-74. The Stallion & Soldier kit is not shown.

Dr. Zaius model kit by Addar, 1973. Mint in Box (MIB): $50-75.
Built: $30-40.

General Ursus model kit by Addar, 1973.
Mint in box (MIB): $50-75. Built: $30-40.

Cornelius model kit by Addar, 1973. Mint in Box (MIB): $50-75.
Built: $30-40.

General Aldo model kit by Addar, 1973.
Mint in box (MIB): $50-75. Built: $30-40.

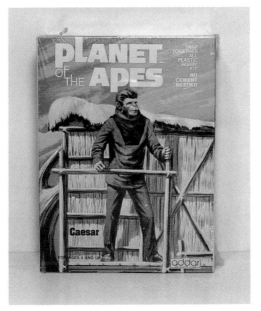

Caesar model kit by Addar, 1974. Mint in
box (MIB): $60-80. Built: $30-40.

Stallion & Soldier model kit by Addar, 1974.
Built: $125-175.

Zira model kit by Addar, 1974. Mint in box
(MIB): $50-75. Built: $30-40.

Stallion & Soldier model kit by Addar, 1974.
Courtesy of Matthew Sotis. Mint in box
(MIB): $200-250.

Scene in a bottle model kits by Addar, 1975.

Cornfield roundup scene in a bottle model kit by Addar, 1975. Mint in box (MIB): $40-60. Built: $20-30.

Treehouse scene in a bottle model kit by Addar, 1975. Mint in box (MIB): $40-60. Built: $ 20 - 30.

Jail wagon scene in a bottle model kit by Addar, 1975. Mint in box (MIB): $40-60. Built: $20-30.

7" Cornelius poly resin statue by an unknown manufacturer, 1996. The statue was made in China and comes painted. $50-75.

Cornelius with ruins model kit by Resins from the Grave, 1995. $100-125.

General Urko resin bust by an unknown manufacturer, 1995. $100-125.

Movie Scripts

Final Production Information Guide on POTA	James Denton	1968	$10-15
Planet of the Apes	Serling/Wilson	1967	$10-15
Beneath the Planet of the Apes	Paul Dehn	1969	$10-15
Escape from the Planet of the Apes	Paul Dehn	1970	$10-15
Conquest of the Planet of the Apes	Paul Dehn	1972	$10-15
Battle for the Planet of the Apes	Paul Dehn	1972	$10-15
Planet of the Men	Pierre Boulle	1968	$10-15
Return to the Planet of the Apes	Elwes/Rifkin	1988	$10-15
(first version from a story by Cassian Elwes and Adam Rifkin)			
The Return of the Apes	Terry Hayes	1995	$10-15

Note: There are several variations to these scripts, especially *Planet* and *Beneath*. *Planet of the Men* and *Return to the Planet of the Apes* were proposed sequels to the original *Planet of the Apes* film. A fourth variation for the sequel to *Planet* was entitled *The Dark Side of the Earth*. *The Return of the Apes* script is the first draft for the proposed remake of *Planet of the Apes*. The prices listed indicate a photocopied version of the script. An original version of the scripts can range from $200-500, depending on the film.

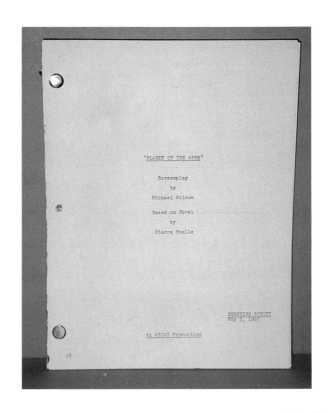

Planet of the Apes movie script by Michael Wilson, 1967. $10-15.

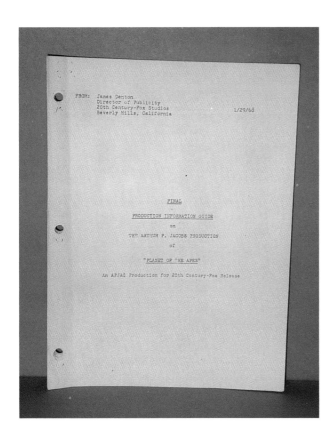

Final Production Information Guide on Planet of the Apes by James Denton, 1968. $10-15.

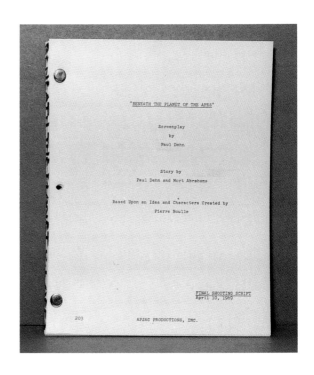

Beneath the Planet of the Apes movie script by Paul Dehn, 1969. $10-15.

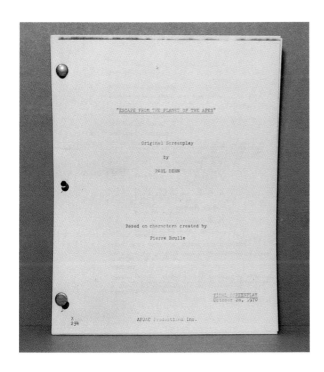

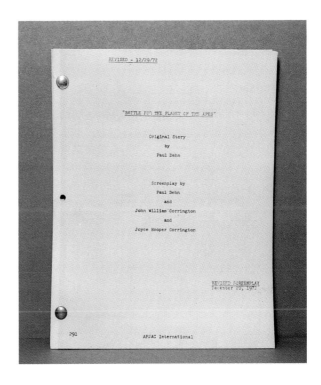

Escape from the Planet of the Apes movie script by Paul Dehn, 1970.
$10-15.

Battle for the Planet of the Apes movie script by Paul Dehn, 1972.
$10-15.

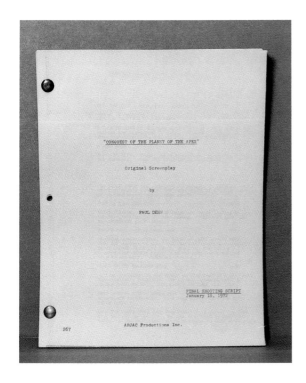

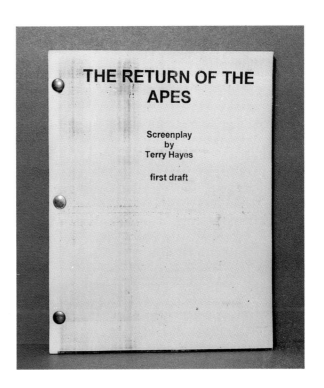

Conquest of the Planet of the Apes movie script by Paul Dehn, 1972.
$10-15.

The Return of the Apes movie script by Terry Hayes, 1995. This was
the first draft written for the proposed remake of *Planet of the Apes*.
$10-15.

Two variations of the *Planet of the Apes* paperback by Pierre Boulle, 1968. $10-15 each.

Paperbacks

Movies

Planet of the Apes	Pierre Boulle	1963	$10-15
Beneath the Planet of the Apes	Michael Avalon	1970	$10-15
Escape from the Planet of the Apes	Jerry Pournelle	1973	$10-15
Conquest of the Planet of the Apes	John Jakes	1973	$10-15
Battle for the Planet of the Apes	David Gerrold	1973	$10-15

Note: *Planet of the Apes* was released with three different cover variations. Two have the same photos from the film, but one says "now an exciting 20th Century Fox motion picture."

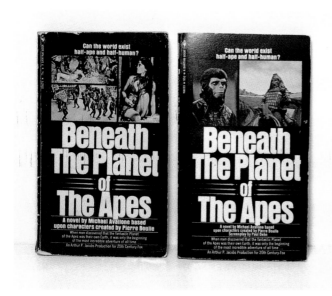

Two variations of the *Beneath the Planet of the Apes* paperback by Michael Avalon, 1970. $10-15 each.

Escape from the Planet of the Apes paperback by Jerry Pournelle, 1973. $10-15.

Conquest of the Planet of the Apes paperback by John Jakes, 1973. $10-15.

Battle for the Planet of the Apes paperback by David Gerrold, 1973. You will notice that the cover for this paperback is actually a scene from Conquest. $10-15.

One has a drawing of an primitive ape on it. *Beneath the Planet of the Apes* was released with two cover variations. There were different photos from the film on each cover.

Television Series

#1 Man the Fugitive	George Effinger	1974	$10-15
#2 Escape to Tomorrow	George Effinger	1974	$10-15
#3 Journey into Terror	George Effinger	1974	$10-15
#4 Lord of the Apes	George Effinger	1974	$10-15

Return to the Planet of the Apes Cartoon

#1 Visions from Nowhere	William Arrow	1974	$10-15
#2 Escape from Terror Lagoon	William Arrow	1976	$10-15
#3 Man, the Hunted Animal	William Arrow	1976	$10-15

Note: The paperbacks from the animated cartoon actually have photos from the television series on the cover, but the stories are from the cartoon.

Three paperbacks from the television series (*#1 Man the Fugitive*, *#2 Escape To Tomorrow*, *#3 Journey into Terror*) by George Effinger, 1974. $10-15 each.

Escape from Terror Lagoon paperback by William Arrow, 1976. Although the photo for this book is from the television series, the story is based on the cartoon. $10-15.

Playsets/Games/Vehicles

Action Jackson Lost Continent	Mego	1974	$300-350
Action Stallion (remote control)	Mego	1974	$125-150
Adventure Set	Amsco	1974	$200-250
Bagatelle (mini pinball game)	Unknown	1974	$75-100
Battering Ram	Mego	1974	$50-75
Boardgame	Milton Bradley	1974	$50-75
Catapult and Wagon	Mego	1974	$50-75
Catapult and Wagon w/horse	Mego	1974	$75-125
Colorforms Adventure Set	Colorforms	1974	$50-75
Color-vue Pencil Coloring Set	Hasbro	1974	$80-100
Forbidden Zone Trap Playset	Mego	1974	$175-225
Fortress Playset	Mego	1974	$175-225
Friction Powered Prison Wagon	AHI	1974	$75-100
General Urko Custom Headquarters	Matt Sotis	1996	$250-300
Helicopter	AHI	1974	$50-75
Jail	Mego	1974	$50-75
Playhouse (five feet tall)	Coleco	1974	$100-200
Mini Playset (small figures)	Multiple Toymakers	1974	$75-125
Playset #1331 (small figures)	Multiple Toymakers	1974	$100-150
Playset #5552 (small figures)	Multiple Toymakers	1974	$100-150
Individual figures from playsets	Multiple Toymakers	1974	$3-5 ea.
Quick Draw Cartoons	Pressman	1973	$50-75
Ring Toss Game	Pressman	1974	$75-100
Rock Launcher	Palitoy	1974	$75-100
Safety Dart Game (w/gorilla target)	Transogram	1974	$75-100
Small Target Set	Multiple	1974	$50-100
Spin N' Color Game	Pressman	1973	$50-75
Stain Glass Craft Kit	Winner Promotions	1974	$50-100
Target Game (w/gun and targets)	Transogram	1974	$100-150
Dr. Zaius Throne	Mego	1974	$50-75
Treehouse Playset	Mego	1974	$150-200
Village Playset	Mego	1974	$200-250

Note: The playsets (Forbidden Zone Trap, Fortress, Treehouse, and Village) were also released in mailing boxes. The Action Jackson Lost Continent playset was marketed as an apes playset, although it really did not relate to the *Planet of the Apes*.

Action stallion (remote control) by Mego, 1974. $125-150.

Adventure set by Amsco, 1974. Mint in box (MIB): $200-250.

Adventure set by Amsco, 1974. Loose and built: $100-125.

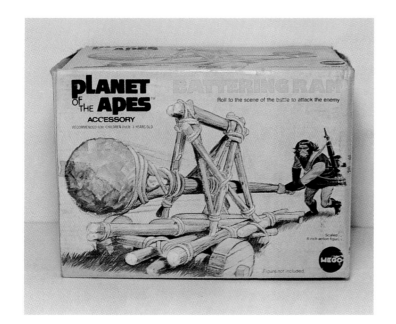

Battering ram by Mego, 1974. $50-75.

Catapult and wagon by Mego, 1974. $50-75.

Boardgame by Milton Bradley, 1974. $50-75.

Board used for the game by Milton Bradley, 1974.

Fortress playset by Mego, 1974. *Courtesy of Matthew Sotis.* $175-225.

Color-vue pencil coloring set by Hasbro, 1974. $80-100.

Colorforms adventure set by Colorforms, 1974. $50-75.

Forbidden zone trap playset by Mego, 1974. *Courtesy of Matthew Sotis.* $175-225.

Friction powered wagon by AHI, 1974. Mint on Card (MOC): $75-100. Loose: $30-50.

Interior of custom General Urko headquarters with a custom gorilla on patrol by Matthew Sotis, 1996. Figure not included. *Courtesy of Matthew Sotis.* $250-300.

Helicopter by AHI, 1974. $50-75.

Exterior of custom General Urko headquarters with Mego and custom figures by Matthew Sotis, 1996. Figures not included. *Courtesy of Matthew Sotis.* $250-300.

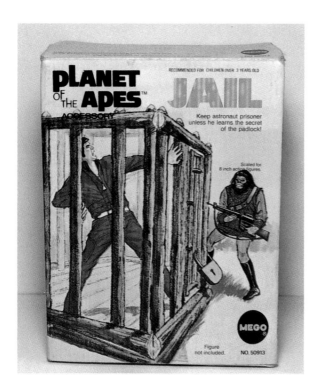

Jail by Mego, 1974. $50-75.

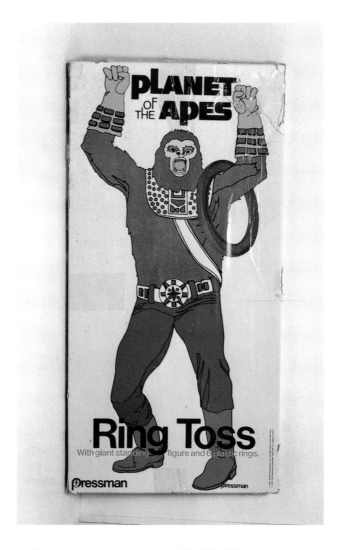

Figures of Dr. Zaius, Zira, and gorilla soldiers from a playset by Multiple Toymakers, 1974. $3-5 each.

Ring toss game by Pressman, 1974. $75-100.

Safety dart game by Transogram, 1974. $75-100.

Spin n' color game by Pressman, 1973. $50-75.

Dr. Zaius throne by Mego, 1974. $50-75.

Small target set by Multiple Toymakers, 1974. $50-100.

Target game by Transogram, 1974. $100-150.

Treehouse playset by Mego, 1974. $150-200.

Posters/Lobby Cards/Pressbooks/ Newspapers

Due to the many varieties and sizes available for this section, I am only listing some of the photos, poster sizes, and pressbooks available with the estimated prices. There were also press-kits produced, but there are few details as to whether they were made for each film. However, the press-kits that were made included a folder, pressbook, newspaper, pre-release guide, synopsis, and lobby cards or stills. Further, the list is exclusively for American products and does not include any foreign merchandise that was produced. The foreign merchandise is a little harder to locate and more expensive than the American merchandise. Some of the foreign posters, however, contain better graphics than the American posters. The following merchandise was produced by 20th Century-Fox in conjunction with the release of each *Planet of the Apes* film.

Planet of the Apes

One Sheet (28"x42")	20th Century-Fox 1968	$150-200
Window Card (14"x22")	20th Century-Fox 1968	$100-150
Insert Card (15"x37")	20th Century-Fox 1968	$75-125
Door Panels	20th Century-Fox 1968	$300-400 ea.
(set of 4)		$1,200-1,500
Lobby Cards	20th Century-Fox 1968	$25-35 ea.
(set of 8 11"x14")		$200-250
Color Stills	20th Century-Fox 1968	$15-20 ea.
(set of 8 8"x10")		$100-125
Pressbook	20th Century-Fox 1968	$150-200
Newspaper Giveaway	20th Century-Fox 1968	$25-50

One sheet (28" x 42") movie poster for *Planet of the Apes* by 20th Century-Fox, 1968. $150-200.

Front of village playset by Mego, 1974. Mint in box (MIB): $200-250. Loose: $100-150.

Back of village playset by Mego, 1974.

Inside of newspaper from *Planet of the Apes*, 1968.

Planet of the Apes pressbook by 20th Century-Fox, 1968. $150-200.

Front of newspaper from *Planet of the Apes* by 20th Century-Fox. The newspaper was given away at theaters and in press kits during the release of the film, 1968. $25-50.

Back of newspaper from *Planet of the Apes*, 1968.

Lobby card from *Planet of the Apes* by 20th Century-Fox, 1996. $25-35.

Lobby card from *Planet of the Apes* by 20th Century-Fox, 1996. $25-35.

Lobby card from *Planet of the Apes* by 20th Century-Fox, 1996. $25-35.

Lobby card from *Planet of the Apes* by 20th Century-Fox, 1996. $25-35.

Lobby card from *Planet of the Apes* by 20th Century-Fox, 1996. $25-35.

Beneath the Planet of the Apes

One Sheet (28"x42")	20th Century-Fox	1970	$75-100
Insert Card (15"x37")	20th Century-Fox	1970	$30-50
Title Card (11"x14")	20th Century-Fox	1970	$25-50
Window Card (14"x22")	20th Century-Fox	1970	$40-60
Lobby Cards	20th Century-Fox	1970	$15-25 ea.
(set of 8 11"x14")			$100-150
Color Stills	20th Century-Fox	1970	$10-15 ea.
(set of 8 8"x10")			$50-75
Pressbook	20th Century-Fox	1970	$40-50
Newspaper Giveaway	20th Century-Fox	1970	$20-40

Lobby card from *Planet of the Apes* by 20th Century-Fox, 1996. $25-35.

Lobby card from *Planet of the Apes* by 20th Century-Fox, 1996. $25-35.

Lobby card from *Planet of the Apes* by 20th Century-Fox, 1996. $25-35.

One sheet (28"x42") movie poster for *Beneath the Planet of the Apes* by 20th Century-Fox, 1970. $75-100.

Newspaper from *Beneath the Planet of the Apes* by 20th Century-Fox, which was given away at theaters and in press kits during the release of the film, 1970. $20-40.

Pressbook from *Beneath the Planet of the Apes* by 20th Century-Fox, 1970. $40-50.

Lobby card from *Beneath the Planet of the Apes* by 20th Century-Fox, 1970. $15-25.

Lobby card from *Beneath the Planet of the Apes* by 20th Century-Fox, 1970. $15-25.

Lobby card from *Beneath the Planet of the Apes* by 20th Century-Fox, 1970. $15-25.

Lobby card from *Beneath the Planet of the Apes* by 20th Century-Fox, 1970. $15-25.

Lobby card from *Beneath the Planet of the Apes* by 20th Century-Fox, 1970. $15-25.

Lobby card from *Beneath the Planet of the Apes* by 20th Century-Fox, 1970. $15-25.

Lobby card from *Beneath the Planet of the Apes* by 20th Century-Fox, 1970. $15-25.

Lobby card from *Beneath the Planet of the Apes* by 20th Century-Fox, 1970. $15-25.

Escape from the Planet of the Apes

One Sheet (28"x42")	20th Century-Fox 1971	$40-60
Half-Sheet (23"x29")	20th Century-Fox 1971	$30-50
Insert Card (15"x37")	20th Century-Fox 1971	$25-50
Title Card (11"x14")	20th Century-Fox 1971	$25-40
Window Card (14"x22")	20th Century-Fox 1971	$30-50
Lobby Cards	20th Century-Fox 1971	$10-15 ea.
(set of 8 11"x14")		$60-80
Color Stills	20th Century-Fox 1971	$5-10 ea.
(set of 8 8"x10")		$30-50
Pressbook	20th Century-Fox 1971	$20-30
Newspaper Giveaway	20th Century-Fox 1971	$15-25
Sheet Music	Charles Hansen 1974	$50-100

Conquest of the Planet of the Apes

One Sheet (28"x42")	20th Century-Fox 1972	$40-60
Half Sheet (23"x29")	20th Century-Fox 1972	$30-50
Insert Card(15"x37")	20th Century-Fox 1972	$25-40
Three sheet	20th Century-Fox 1972	$60-80
Six Sheet	20th Century-Fox 1972	$75-100
Twenty-Four Sheet	20th Century-Fox 1972	$100-150
Lobby Cards	20th Century-Fox 1972	$10-15 ea.
(set of 8 11"x14")		$60-80
Color Stills	20th Century-Fox 1972	$5-10 ea.
(set of 8 8"x10")		$30-40
Pressbook	20th Century-Fox 1972	$20-30
Newspaper Giveaway	20th Century-Fox 1972	$15-25

One sheet (28" x 42") movie poster for *Escape from the Planet of the Apes* by 20th Century-Fox, 1971. $40-60.

Lobby card from *Escape from the Planet of the Apes* by 20th Century-Fox, 1971. $10-15.

One sheet (28" x 42") movie poster for *Conquest of the Planet of the Apes* by 20th Century-Fox, 1972. $40-60.

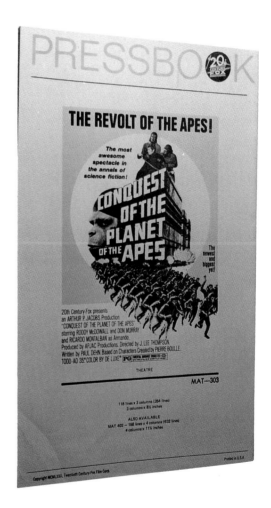

Pressbook from *Conquest of the Planet of the Apes* by 20th Century-Fox, 1972. $20-30.

Lobby card from *Conquest of the Planet of the Apes* by 20th Century-Fox, 1972. $10-15.

Lobby card from *Conquest of the Planet of the Apes* by 20th Century-Fox, 1972. $10-15.

Lobby card from *Conquest of the Planet of the Apes* by 20th Century-Fox, 1972. $10-15.

Lobby card from *Conquest of the Planet of the Apes* by 20th Century-Fox, 1972. $10-15.

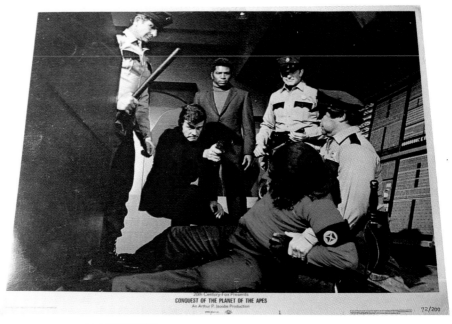

Lobby card from *Conquest of the Planet of the Apes* by 20th Century-Fox, 1972. $10-15.

Lobby card from *Conquest of the Planet of the Apes* by 20th Century-Fox, 1972. $10-15.

Lobby card from *Conquest of the Planet of the Apes* by 20th
Century-Fox, 1972. $10-15.

Lobby card from *Conquest of the Planet of the Apes* by 20th
Century-Fox, 1972. $10-5.

Battle for the Planet of the Apes

One Sheet (28"x42")	20th Century-Fox 1973	$30-50
Insert Card (15"x37")	20th Century-Fox 1973	$20-40
Six Sheet	20th Century-Fox 1973	$75-100
Twenty-Four Sheet (teaser)	20th Century-Fox 1973	$100-150
Lobby Cards	20th Century-Fox 1973	$10-15 ea.
(set of 8 11"x14")		$60-80
Color Stills	20th Century-Fox 1973	$5-10 ea.
(set of 8 8"x10")		$30-40
Pressbook	20th Century-Fox 1973	$20-30
Newspaper Giveaway	20th Century-Fox 1973	$15-25

Pressbook from *Battle for the Planet of the Apes* by 20th Century-Fox, 1973. $20-30.

One sheet (28" x 42") movie poster from *Battle for the Planet of the Apes* by 20th Century-Fox, 1973. $30-50.

Newspaper from *Battle for the Planet of the Apes* by 20th Century-Fox, which was giveaway at theaters and in press kits during the release of the film, 1973. $15-25.

Lobby card from *Battle for the Planet of the Apes* by 20th Century-Fox, 1973. $10-15.

More Ape Posters, Etc.

Planet of the Apes mini-poster in lucite	20th Century-Fox	1994	$15-30
(this poster was sold exclusively on QVC)			
Planet/Beneath Combo Poster	20th Century-Fox	1970	$100-125
Planet/Beneath Combo Pressbook	20th Century-Fox	1970	$30-50
Go Ape One Sheet (28"x42")	20th Century-Fox	1974	$100-125
Go Ape Insert Card (15"x37")	20th Century-Fox	1974	$40-60
Go Ape Pressbook	20th Century-Fox	1974	$20-40
Go Ape Cloth Patch (Dr. Zaius)	20th Century-Fox	1974	$10-20
Video Poster	CBS/Fox	1990	$30-50
(features all five movies from video release)			
Corneilus Poster (16"x20")	20th Century-Fox	1994	$10-20
(this poster was sold exclusively on QVC)			
Meet Zira and Cornelius Brochure	20th Century-Fox	1974	$40-60
(live appearances brochure with publicity shots)			
Fan Card w/Burke, Virdon, & Galen	20th Century-Fox	1974	$10-20

Note: The prices listed above refer to items in mint to near mint condition. As the condition grade decreases, so will the price. It is very difficult to find any of the posters rolled, except for the video poster, but you can still find folded posters in excellent condition. It is tough to find the lobby card sets in mint condition for *Planet* and *Beneath*, but the lobby card sets for the other films are more common. Also, the *Go Ape* promotion was a collaboration between 20th Century-Fox and Mego. The material that was released for this promotion will either say "20th Century-Fox wants you to *Go Ape*", "Mego wants you to *Go Ape*", or "20th Century-Fox and Mego want you to *Go Ape*".

One sheet (28" x 42") combo movie poster for *Planet of the Apes & Beneath the Planet of the Apes* when they were released at drive-in theaters as a double feature by 20th Century-Fox, 1970. $100-125.

Poster from video release by 20th Century-Fox, 1990. $30-50.

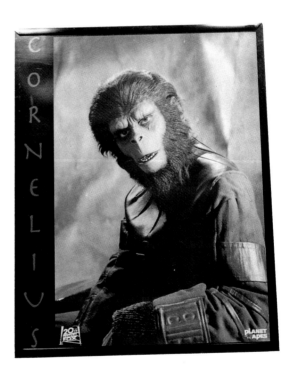

Cornelius poster (16" x 20") which was sold on QVC by 20th Century-Fox, 1994. $10-20.

Pressbook from *Go Ape* promotion by 20th Century-Fox, 1974. $20-40.

Brochure from *Meet Zira and Cornelius* promotion by 20th Century-Fox, 1974. $40-60.

Puzzles

Cornelius, Zira, Lucius (box)	H.G. Toys	1974	$15-25
General Aldo on Patrol (box)	H.G. Toys	1974	$15-25
General Aldo (box)	H.G. Toys	1974	$15-25
Cornelius, Zira, Lucius (canister)	H.G. Toys	1974	$15-25
General Aldo on Patrol (canister)	H.G. Toys	1974	$15-25
General Aldo (canister)	H.G. Toys	1974	$15-25
Battle for the Planet of the Apes	H.G. Toys	1974	$50-75
The Chase	H.G. Toys	1974	$50-75
Dr. Zaius Poster Puzzle	Aurora	1974	$50-75
Galen Poster Puzzle	Aurora	1974	$50-75
General Urko and Soldier	Whitman	1974	$125-150
General Urko and Burke	Whitman	1974	$125-150
Genral Urko and Dr. Zaius	Whitman	1974	$125-150
Caesar, Virgil, and Lisa	Whitman	1974	$125-150

Note: The box and canister puzzles of Cornelius, Zira, and Lucius are errors. The picture is actually Caesar, Lisa, and young Cornelius from *Battle for the Planet of the Apes*. The Whitman puzzles are imported from Britain.

Box puzzle of Cornelius, Zira, and Lucius by H.G. Toys, 1974. The photo for this puzzle is actually Caesar, Lisa, and young Cornelius from *Battle for the Planet of the Apes*. $15-25.

Box puzzle of General Aldo "On Patrol" by H.G. Toys, 1974. $15-25.

Canister puzzles by H.G. Toys, 1974.

Canister puzzle of General Aldo by H.G. Toys, 1974. $15-25.

Canister puzzle of Cornelius, Zira, and Lucius by H.G. Toys, 1974. The photo for this puzzle is actually Caesar, Lisa, and young Cornelius from *Battle for the Planet of the Apes*. $15-25.

Canister puzzle of General Aldo "On Patrol" by H.G. Toys, 1974. $15-25.

Dr. Zaius poster puzzle by Aurora, 1974. $50-75.

Battle for the Planet of Apes puzzle by H.G. Toys, 1974. $50-75.

Galen poster puzzle by Aurora, 1974. $50-75.

The Chase puzzle by H.G. Toys, 1974. $50-75.

Records/Compact Discs

Planet of the Apes Soundtrack (33 1/3)	Total Sound	1968	$50-75
Planet of the Apes Soundtrack (compact disc)	Project 3	1990	$5-10
Planet of the Apes Soundtrack (compact disc) (includes the previously unreleased track, *The Hunt*)	Intrada	1993	$20-25
Beneath the Planet of the Apes Soundtrack (33 1/3)	Amos Records	1970	$100-150
Themes from Star Trek, POTA T.V. (33 1/3 Album)	AA Records	1975	$50-75
Album #8147 (33 1/3) (Planet, Beneath, Escape, Battle)	Power Records	1974	$50-75
Album #8148 (33 1/3) (*Mountain of Delphi*)	Power Records	1974	$50-75
Album (33 1/3) (*Planet of the Apes*: a musical trip with Don Posts masks)	Terry Philips	1974	$50-100
Album (33 1/3) (themes from '70s TV shows including *Planet of the Apes*)	AA Records	1976	$35-75
Record (45) (*Dawn of Tree People*)	Power Records	1974	$15-35
Record (45) (*Mountain of Delphi*)	Power Records	1974	$15-35
Record (45) (*Battle of Two Worlds*)	Power Records	1974	$15-35
Record (45) (*Apes Shuffle*)	AA Records	1974	$15-35
Radio spots from all five movies (45 records for each film)	20th Century-Fox	1974	$20-30 ea.

Note: The Project 3 compact disc was released without the first notes for the *Main Title* track. This error is not present on the LP release. It also doesn't have as wide a stereo image as the re-mastered Intrada release.

Planet of the Apes soundtrack on compact disc by Project3, 1990. $5-10.

Planet of the Apes soundtrack on compact disc by Intrada, 1993. This version contains the previously unreleased track, *The Hunt*. $20-25.

Planet of the Apes soundtrack by Total Sound, 1968. $50-75.

Beneath the Planet of the Apes soundtrack by Amos Records, 1970. *Courtesy of Matthew Sotis. $100-150.*

Record album with stories for *Planet, Beneath, Escape* and *Battle* by Power Records, 1974. $50-75.

Themes from Star Trek, Planet of the Apes television series record by A.A. Records, 1975. $50-75.

Mountain of Delphi 45 record by Power Records, 1974. $15-35.

Planet of the Apes and *Beneath the Planet of the Apes* Super 8 films by Ken Films, 1974. $50-75 and $25-50 respectively.

Mountain of Delphi album by Power Records, 1974. $50-75.

Super 8 Films/View-Masters

Planet of the Apes	Ken Films	1974	$50-75
Beneath the Planet of the Apes	Ken Films	1974	$25-50
Escape from the Planet of the Apes	Ken Films	1974	$25-50
Conquest of the Planet of the Apes	Ken Films	1974	$25-50
Battle for the Planet of the Apes	Ken Films	1974	$25-50
Beneath the Planet of the Apes View-Master Test Reels	GAF	1970	$200-400
View-Master (Silent)	GAF	1974	$30-50
View-Master (Talking)	GAF	1974	$40-75
View-Master (Canadian/ Bi-Lingual)	GAF	1974	$100-200
View-Master (German/Silent)	GAF	1974	$100-200
View-Master (11" Italian Storybook)	GAF	1974	$20-40

Silent and talking view-master sets by GAF, 1974. $30-50 and $40-75 respectively.

Note: The Super 8 films were released in color and black & white. The above prices are for the black & white versions. The color versions are rarer; therefore, the prices are slightly higher.

The *Beneath* View-Master contained five test reels. It was never released to the public due to the violent nature of some of the images.

Escape from the Planet of the Apes, *Conquest of the Planet of the Apes*, and *Battle for the Planet of the Apes* Super 8 films by Ken Films, 1974. $25-50.

A different variation of the Caesar, Lisa, and Cornelius t-shirt from *Battle for the Planet of the Apes* by Mosquitohead, 1996. $20-25.

Caesar, Lisa, and Cornelius t-shirt from *Battle for the Planet of the Apes* by Mosquitohead, 1995. $20-25.

T-Shirts/Iron-ons (Licensed & Unlicensed)

Battle Family Portrait (black) (Caesar, Lisa, Cornelius)	Mosquitohead	1995	$20-25
General Ursus (black) (Monkey See, Monkey Do)	Unknown	1995	$20-25
Gorillas in Stadium (black) (Beneath written in neon green)	Unknown	1995	$20-25
Color photos of Caesar, Aldo, Zaius, & Cornelius (black)	Fuct	1995	$20-25
Planet Movie Poster on front of shirt (black)	Unknown	1995	$25-30
(General Ursus with Monkey See, Monkey Do on the back of a long sleeve shirt.)			
Planet POTA logo only (white)	Mosquitohead	1995	$20-25
Marcus (white)	Mosquitohead	1995	$20-25
Gorillas in Stadium (white) (*Planet of the Apes* logo in red)	Mosquitohead	1995	$20-25
Cornelius and Zira kissing (white) (*Planet of the Apes* logo above picture)	Unknown	1996	$15-20
Gorilla Soldier head shot (white) (*Planet of the Apes* logo above picture)	Unknown	1996	$15-20
Sacred Scrolls (black) (w/back of Statue of Liberty head shot & POTA logo in red)	Unknown	1996	$20-25
Dr. Zaius w/Lawgiver (white) ("Ape shall not harm Ape" caption)	Mosquitohead	1996	$20-25
Go Ape Poster (black)	Mosquitohead	1996	$20-25
Dr. Zaius (black) (small picture with "made on planet earth")	Fuct	1996	$20-25
Cornelius (brown) (small picture with "made on planet earth")	Fuct	1996	$20-25
Comic/Magazine Cover #1 (yellow)	Unknown	1996	$20-25
Comic/Magazine Cover #2 (yellow)	Unknown	1996	$20-25
Comic/Magazine Cover #3 (yellow)	Unknown	1996	$20-25

Comic/Magazine Cover #4 (yellow)	Unknown	1996	$20-25
Comic/Magazine Cover #7 (yellow)	Unknown	1996	$20-25
Comic/Magazine Cover #21 (light blue)	Unknown	1996	$20-25
Mad Magazine Cover (yellow)	Unknown	1996	$15-20
Movie Monsters Dr. Zaius Cover (cream)	Unknown	1996	$15-20
Video Advertisement (cream)	Unknown	1996	$20-25
T.V. Week Magazine Cover (yellow)	Unknown	1996	$25-30
Planet of the Apes Teachers Guide Cover (yellow)	Unknown	1996	$25-30
World of Horror Cover (yellow)	Unknown	1996	$20-25
Zira "Human See, Human Do" caption (black)	Mosquitohead	1996	$20-25
General Urko (smoking bong)	Unknown	1995	$20-25
Dr. Zaius on header card	Werby Industries	1974	$75-100
Three Apes on puffy style decal	Pilgrim	1974	$75-100
Caesar on puffy style decal	Shirtees	1974	$75-100
Galen Iron-on	Roach Company	1974	$15- 25
Dr. Zaius Iron-on	Roach Company	1974	$15-25

Note: The *Battle for the Planet of the Apes* family portrait (Caesar, Lisa, and Cornelius) shirt is also available in white with a frame border around the photo. Also, although most of the above T-shirts were released in the two years prior to this writing, several were made in limited quantity and are, therefore, difficult to locate.

Stadium scene t-shirt with *Planet of the Apes* logo in red by Mosquitohead, 1995. $20-25.

Stadium scene from *Beneath the Planet of the Apes* t-shirt by an unknown manufacturer, 1995. $20-25.

Photos of Cornelius, Dr. Zaius, General Aldo, and Caesar t-shirt by an unknown manufacturer, 1995. $20-25.

Planet of the Apes movie poster t-shirt by an unknown manufacturer, 1995. $25-30.

Back of movie poster t-shirt by an unknown manufacturer, 1995. This design was also available as the front of a black, short sleeve t-shirt. The price range for the short sleeve shirt is $20-25.

Planet of the Apes logo t-shirt by Mosquitohead, 1995. $20-25.

Marcus t-shirt by Mosquitohead, 1995. $20-25.

Drawing of Cornelius and Zira kissing t-shirt by an unknown manufacturer, 1996. $15-20.

Drawing of a gorillas head t-shirt by an unknown manufacturer, 1996. $15-20.

View from behind the Statue of Liberty with a passage from the Sacred Scrolls t-shirt by an unknown manufacturer, 1996. $20-25.

Dr. Zaius with the Lawgiver in the background t-shirt by
Mosquitohead, 1996. $20-25.

Go Ape movie poster t-shirt by Mosquitohead, 1996. $20-25.

Zira t-shirt by Mosquitohead, 1996. $20-25.

Small drawing of Dr. Zaius' head t-shirt by Fuct, 1996. $20-25.

Small drawing of Cornelius' head t-shirt by Fuct, 1996. $20-25.

Dr. Zaius on the cover of *Movie Monsters* magazine t-shirt by an unknown manufacturer, 1996, $15-20.

Galen, Burke, and Virdon on the cover of *T.V. Week* t-shirt by an
unknown manufacturer, 1996, $25-30.

Video advertisement t-shirt for the ape films by an unknown
manufacturer, 1996, $20-25.

Cover of *Planet of the Apes* comic magazine #1 t-shirt by an
unknown manufacturer, 1996, $20-25.

Cover of *Planet of the Apes* comic magazine #21 t-shirt by an
unknown manufacturer, 1996. $20-25.

Galen iron-on transfer on a t-shirt by Roach Company, 1974. $15-25.

Dr. Zaius iron-on by Roach Company, 1974. $15-25.

Movie gum card display box by Topps, 1968. $125-150.

Trading Cards

Movie Gum Card Box (24 packs)	Topps, Inc.	1968	$700-900
Movie Gum Card Display Box	Topps, Inc.	1968	$125-150
Movie Gum Card Set (1-44)	Topps, Inc.	1968	$150-200
Movie Unopened Pack	Topps, Inc.	1968	$30-50
Movie Wrapper	Topps, Inc.	1968	$20-30
Individual Cards from Movie Set	Topps, Inc.	1968	$5-10
TV Gum Card Box (36 packs)	Topps, Inc.	1974	$125-200
TV Gum Card Display Box	Topps, Inc.	1974	$50-75
TV Gum Card Set (1-66)	Topps, Inc.	1974	$50-75
TV Unopened Pack	Topps, Inc.	1974	$15-25
TV Wrapper	Topps, Inc.	1974	$10-15
Individual Cards from TV Set	Topps, Inc.	1974	$3-5
British Wrapper	ABC Chewing	1960s	$40-60
British Movie Card Set (1-44)	ABC Chewing	1960s	$200-250

Note: The British card set is smaller than the Topps version and the cards contain a black border around them.

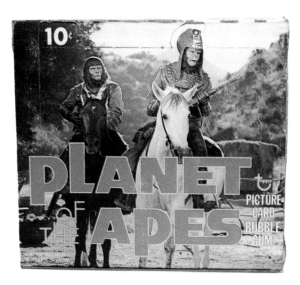

Television series gum card display box by Topps, 1974. $50-75.

Unopened packs of cards from the film and television series by Topps, 1968 & 1974. $30-50 and $15-25 respectively.

Gum card wrapper from the film by Topps, 1968. $20-30.

Planet of the Apes cards from the film by Topps, 1968. Complete set of 44 cards: $150-200. Individual cards: $5-10.

British gum card wrapper for *Planet of the Apes* by ABC Chewing, 1970s. $40-60.

Planet of the Apes cards from the film by Topps, 1968.

Planet of the Apes cards from the film by Topps, 1968.

Back of cards from the film by Topps, 1968.

Planet of the Apes cards from the television series by Topps, 1974.
Complete set of 66 cards: $50-75. Individual cards: $3-5. Please take
note that this set is missing card #58.

Planet of the Apes cards from the television series by Topps, 1974.

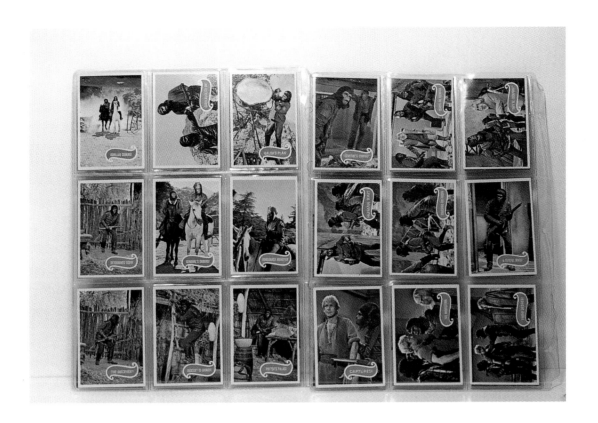

Planet of the Apes cards from the television series by Topps, 1974.

Planet of the Apes cards from the television series by Topps, 1974.

Planet of the Apes and *Beneath the Planet of the Apes* videos by CBS/Fox, 1990. $15-20.

Escape from the Planet of the Apes, Conquest of the Planet of the Apes, and *Battle for the Planet of the Apes* videos by CBS/Fox, 1990. $15-20.

TV Guides

Fall Preview 1973 (movie premiere)	*TV Guide*	1973	$10-20
Fall Preview 1974 (television series premiere)	*TV Guide*	1974	$10-20
*September 14 - December 15, 1974	*TV Guide*	1974	$5-10

* - These are all the issues when the television series was originally aired.

Note: The above issues contain listings on the first film and television series. *Planet of the Apes* has never appeared on the cover of TV Guide.

Videos — Movies

Planet of the Apes	CBS/Fox	1990	$15-20
Beneath the Planet of the Apes	CBS/Fox	1990	$15-20
Escape from the Planet of the Apes	CBS/Fox	1990	$15-20
Conquest of the Planet of the Apes	CBS/Fox	1990	$15-20
Battle for the Planet of the Apes	CBS/Fox	1990	$15-20

Note: I have learned from a fellow ape collector that 20th Century-Fox is going to be releasing a box set of the videos with THX sound for the original five films. The movies are also being re-released on laser disc, but *Battle for the Planet of the Apes* will not be included. No release date was available at the time this book was written.

Television Series (14 episodes)	CBS/Fox	1974	$10-15 ea.

(Broadcast on Friday evenings at 8:00 PM on CBS from 9/13/74-12/20/74)

TV Episodes

Escape from Tomorrow	(Broadcast 9/13/74)
The Gladiators	(Broadcast 9/20/74)
The Trap	(Broadcast 9/27/74)
The Good Seeds	(Broadcast 10/4/74)
The Legacy	(Broadcast 10/11/74)
Tomorrow's Tide	(Broadcast 10/18/74)
The Surgeon	(Broadcast 10/25/74)
The Deception	(Broadcast 11/1/74)
The Horse Race	(Broadcast 11/8/74)
The Interrogation	(Broadcast 11/15/74)
The Tyrant	(Broadcast 11/15/74)
The Cure	(Broadcast 11/29/74)
The Liberator	(Broadcast 12/6/74)
Up Above the World So High	(Broadcast 12/20/74)

Re-Edited TV Series made into TV Movies	CBS/Fox	1970s	$10-15 ea.

TV Movie Titles

Back to the Planet of the Apes
Forgotten City of the Planet of the Apes
Treachery and Greed on the Planet of the Apes
Life, Liberty, and the Pursuit on the Planet of the Apes
Farewell to the Planet of the Apes

Note: CBS/Fox re-edited ten episodes from the television series into five, 2-hour television movies, which they sold to networks for syndication.

Return to the Planet of the Apes NBC   1975 $10-15 ea.

(The 13 episode animated cartoon series was broadcast Saturday mornings on NBC from September 6, 1975-September 4, 1976.)

Cartoon Episodes

Flames of Doom
Escape from Ape City
The Unearthly Prophecy
Tunnel of Fear
Lagoon of Peril
Terror on Ice Mountain
River of Flames
Screaming Wings
Trail of the Unknown
Attack from the Clouds

Mission of Mercy
Invasion of the Underdwellers
Battle of the Titans
A Date with Judy

Note: The story for the fourteenth episode (*A Date with Judy*) appears in the paperback novel of the animated series, but it was never filmed.

Movie Trailers   20th Century-Fox 1970s $10-15

Note: The trailers for the films were done in different time lengths. They were done in 15 second, 30 second, one minute and 90 second spots.

Makeup Screen Test   20th Century-Fox 1970s $10-15

Note: This was the five minute screen test, starring Charlton Heston and Edward G. Robinson, used by Arthur Jacobs to try and convince 20th Century-Fox to fund the making of the film. It also includes pre-production drawings of different scenes for the proposed film.

That's Hollywood Special on
    Planet of the Apes   Unknown   1970s $10-15

Note: This 30 minute special, hosted by Tom Bosley, features behind the scenes action, interviews, makeup tricks, and scenes from all the *Planet of the Apes* films.

Conclusion

The world of *Planet of the Apes* collectibles does not end here. There were several other products produced for this classic science fiction series. Props from the movies and television series are not mentioned in this guide. In my travels, I have come to learn that there are many props available for the films and television series. These items include rifles, pistols, costumes, facial appliances, and masks. As far as the authenticity of these pieces, you can only take the word of the person selling you the item, unless you can obtain a letter of authenticity. I would recommend that you be very selective so you don't get stuck with a piece of worthless merchandise. I also feel that the market for these items is highly overpriced and I would have a tough time purchasing any of these items without a letter of authenticity. For example, a costume from one of the films can demand as much as $4,000, but most of them range between $2,000-3,000. The facial appliances range between $500-1,000 and the prop rifles are worth $500-800. Since you can expect to pay premium money for one of these items, I would advise you to be cautious when purchasing any props from the films or television series. If you do pick an authentic prop, it would make a great addition to any ape collection.

It should also be noted that other licensed merchandise was produced, including bed sheets, blankets, sweatshirts, and polo shirts, but I do not have them or know anyone who has been able to locate them. The sweatshirt and polo shirt were released in the 1970s and manufactured by Pilgrim Sports. Also, there are a large assortment of both color and black & white 8 x 10 stills as well as color transparencies available for all the films, television series, and animated cartoon. The photos can be found both signed and unsigned for all the movies and the television show. The prices vary for signed photos, but for unsigned photos, you shouldn't expect to pay more than $3 for black & white and $5 for color. You have to be careful, however, when you obtain autographs. I would advise you to either obtain the autograph in person, or make sure you receive a letter of authenticity. Collecting animated cels from the *Return to the Planet of the Apes* cartoon is growing in popularity. There are various cels, produced by Filmation, available ranging in price from $200 to $600 each. Some of these cels include a full head shot of a gorilla warrior, General Urko, Cornelius, Zira & two astronauts, and a gorilla reading a book.

Finally, with the anticipated release of a new apes film, comes the anticipation of a new line of ape collectibles. Let's keep our fingers crossed that the new film becomes a reality and inspires the release of a whole new line of ape merchandise. However, even if a new film is not made, you can still find hours of enjoyment watching the original films, television series, and cartoons, as well as collecting memorabilia from them. I hope you enjoyed this in-depth look into the world of *Planet of the Apes* as much a I enjoyed putting it together. Thank you for taking the time to read this book and remember to always keep your eyes open for bargains when searching for those missing pieces of your collection!

Endnotes

1 Denton, James. "Synopsis," *Final Production Guide on Planet of the Apes*. Twentieth Century/Fox. 1968. 3-5.

2 Leader, William, Phd. *Planet of the Apes: A Guide and Commentary for Teachers and Students, Pursuing the study of man.* 1.

3 Winogura, Dale. "Dialogues on Apes, Apes and more Apes," *Cinefantastique*. 1972. 37.

4 Asch, Andrew. "Ape politic," part of "Retrospective/ Monkey Business: The selling of *Planet of the Apes*." *Sci-Fi Universe*. 1994. 37-38.

5 Denton, "Synopsis", 10.

6 Asch, "Ape politic," 34, 39, 41.

7 Moschovitz, Philip. "How they filmed *Planet of the Apes*." *Castle of Frankenstein*. 1969. 22-23.

8 Denton, "Synopsis," 9.

9 Denton, "Synopsis," 10.

10 Quoted in Winogura, "Dialogues," 35.

11 Quoted in Winogura, "Dialogues," 30.

12 Langdon, Verne. "Mad, Mad, Mad Monkey World." *Famous Monsters of Filmland*. Warren Publishing. 1968. 51.

13 Quoted in Winogura, "Dialogues," 35.

14 Quoted in Winogura, "Dialogues," 29.

15 Quoted in Winogura, "Dialogues," 34.

16 Quoted in Winogura, "Dialogues," 31.

17 Asch, "Ape politic," 39.

18 Denton, "Synopsis," 4.

19 Quoted in Winogura, "Dialogues," 30.

20 Heston, Charlton. *In the Arena: An Autobiography.* Simon & Schuster. 1995. p. 394-396.

21 Asch, "Ape politic," 36.

22 Asch, "Ape politic," 36.

23 Lightman, Herb. "Filming Planet of the Apes." *American Cinematographer*. 1968. 259.

Bibliography

Trivia Section

Asch, Andrew. "Ape politic," part of "Retrospective/Monkey Business: The selling of *Planet of the Apes*." *Sci-Fi Universe* (June/July 1994).

Boulle, Pierre. *Planet of the Apes*. Trans Xan Fielding. New York: Signet Books, 1963.

Denton, James. "Synopsis," *Final Production Information Guide on Planet of the Apes*. Twentieth Century-Fox. 1968.

Greene, Eric. *Planet of the Apes as American Myth: Race & Politics in the films and television series.* McFarland & Company, Inc. 1996.

Leader, William, Phd. *Planet of the Apes: A Guide and Commentary for Teachers and Students, Pursuing the study of Man.*

Lightman, Herb. "Filming Planet of the Apes." American Cinematographer. April 1968.

Monroe, Paul. "Review of Return to the Planet of the Apes." *Epilog Magazine*. March 1993.

Planet of the Apes British Annual. Brown Watson. 1975.

Planet of the Apes Video. CBS/Fox. 1990.

Russo, Joe and Larry Landsman with Edward Gross. "Plant of the Apes Revisited." *Starlog* #105 (April 1986): 42-47.

Valerio, Mike. "Art, Commerce and the Planet of the Apes." *Planet of the Apes Official Movie Adaptation*, Malibu Graphics, Inc., 1990.

Wilson, Michael. *Planet of the Apes* screenplay. APJAC Productions & Twentieth Century-Fox. 1967.

Winogura, Dale. "Dialogues on Apes, Apes and more Apes". *Cinefantastique* (Summer 1972): 16-37.

Collectibles Guide

Electronic Arts. "Twentieth Century-Fox Home" (March 21, 1996).

Farr, Joe. *Planet of the Apes* Collectors List. 1996.

George, Anthony. *Planet of the Apes* Collectors List. 1996-1997.

Korbeck, Sharon. "Custom Figures Dwarf Mego's 1970s *Planet of the Apes* Line," *Toy Shop Magazine*. November 8, 1996.

Sandberg, Michael. *Toys in the Attic*. Phoenix, Arizona, 1995.

Sotis, Matthew. Custom *Planet of the Apes* Mego Figures and Masks. 1995-1997.

Sutton, Chris. Custom *Planet of the Apes* Mego Figures. 1995-1996.

Tumbusch, Tom. *Space Adventure Collectibles*. Radnor, Pennsylvania: Wallace-Homestead, 1990.

Index